COUNTRY LIVING

Barefoot Summers

COUNTRY LIVING

Barefoot Summers

REFLECTIONS ON HOME, FAMILY, AND SIMPLE PLEASURES

Faith Andrews Bedford
Illustrations by Scott Baldwin

HEARST BOOKS
A Division of Sterling Publishing Co., Inc.
New York

To Bob

"Plus qu'hier et moins que demain"

Library of Congress Cataloging-in-Publication Data
Bedford, Faith Andrews.
Country living barefoot summers : reflections on home, family, and simple pleasures
/ Faith Andrews Bedford.
p. cm. Includes index.
ISBN 1-58816-451-9
1. Home economics, Rural—United States—Anecdotes. 2. Country life—United States—
Anecdotes. 3. Bedford, Faith Andrews—Anecdotes. I. Title: Barefoot summers. II. Country living
(New York, N.Y.) III. Title.
TX295.B44 2005
640'.973—dc22   2004020053

10 9 8 7 6 5 4 3 2 1

Published by Hearst Books
A Division of Sterling Publishing Co., Inc.
387 Park Avenue South, New York, NY 10016

Country Living is a trademark owned by Hearst Magazines Property, Inc., in USA,
and Hearst Communications, Inc., in Canada. Hearst Books is a trademark
owned by Hearst Communications, Inc.

BOOK DESIGN BY ALEXANDRA MALDONADO

www.countryliving.com

For information about custom editions, special sales, premium and
corporate purchases, please contact Sterling Special Sales Department at
800-805-5489 or specialsales@sterlingpub.com.

Distributed in Canada by Sterling Publishing
c/o Canadian Manda Group, 165 Dufferin Street
Toronto, Ontario, Canada M6K 3H6

Distributed in Australia by Capricorn Link (Australia) Pty. Ltd.
P.O. Box 704, Windsor, NSW 2756 Australia

Printed in China

ISBN 1-58816-451-9

Contents

Section II – As a Mother

Section III – As a Grandmother

Foreword

The sweet smell of bed linens dried on a line in the sun. Ice cold lemonade on a hot summer's day. The comforting sounds an old house makes when it's settling in for a thunderstorm. Why is it that such ordinary things often bring us extraordinary pleasure? Why—in a world full of hi-tech entertainment—do we treasure the memories of quiet, everyday things like taking a walk with a child or watching a flower grow?

Those were the things that filled my life twenty years ago. Woven into the satisfying moments and joyous chaos of raising three children were mornings spent as a breastfeeding consultant at the local hospital. Our life in a little village at the foot of the Blue Ridge Mountains, where I tended a small herb and honey farm, was rich and satisfying. I was content. Then one day, my husband, a professor at the nearby university, told us he'd been offered a job in New York City. Seeing the stricken look on my face, he assured me that it was only for a couple of years and that we would, of course, keep the farm.

With our two oldest children, Drew and Eleanor, in college and our youngest, Sarah, eager for a new adventure, we set off for life in the big city. Inspired to explore new directions for myself as well, I returned to school and began researching the American Impressionist painter, Frank W. Benson. In the midst of all this, as a peaceful interlude between classes and intensive research sessions, I began writing short stories and essays about life in the country where traditions run deep and memories bind the generations together.

I found myself reflecting on quiet pursuits and simple pleasures, remembering ordinary, everyday things—things that often escape our notice. Some stories spoke of the modest triumphs of children, others were about the security in customs that were once taken for granted. Some were about my children; others about my own childhood years. When we left New York and returned to the farm I continued writing these stories, for the wellspring of ideas and subjects seemed endless.

As a lark, I submitted an essay about buying my first pickup truck to *Ms. Magazine*. They accepted it immediately. Emboldened by this success, I sent a piece to *Country Living* about the lemonade stands my sisters and I used to have every Fourth of July. It was perfect for the magazine, said Marjorie Gage, my first editor, and she asked for more. My column, "Kids in the Country," is now a regular feature.

I now balance my love of writing about the simple pleasures of rural life with my work as an art historian. My initial research on Frank Benson became the biographical essay for a Benson retrospective in Manhattan. A biography, a second book, and numerous articles on the artist followed. I co-curated a Benson exhibition and now travel across the country lecturing on his life and times.

But writing a book on art may take years to research and finally see in print, while essays can be written in a week and appear in just a few months. I love doing both and find each to be deeply satisfying.

I am often asked if I shall ever run out of ideas for essays. Never! My only frustration is that I will not live long enough to get them all down on paper. Everywhere I turn stories present themselves. A word, the sight of geese against an autumn sky, a snatch of song, a glimpse of children playing a game—these and a host of other things beg to be written down. And when readers tell me that something I have written has touched them deeply, inspired a new tradition, caused them to pause and take time to remember, I am delighted.

These days, I am asked to speak on writing as often as on art. Since my essays are really mini-memoirs, I urge my listeners to create their own. Everyone longs to know more about those they love. And through writing we can capture the memories of the little things that define us and tell others who we are. I especially enjoy working with hospice patients, senior citizens, and nursing home residents. It is rewarding to help them express their wonderful wealth of stories and memories.

A few months before the birth of our first grandchild, I ran into an old friend. I confessed to being a bit nervous in the new role and asked him what being a grandparent truly means. "A grandparent," he told me solemnly, "is someone who tells the stories." And so I do.

Faith Andrews Bedford

Acknowledgments

To the readers who asked for more stories: Here they are. To my family and friends, who have inspired these essays and given me much support, thank you. And to my editors at *Country Living*—Tom Claire, Marjorie Gage, and Lyn Konstantin—who smoothed the rough edges of my stories, and to Lee Fowler, who helped shape this book, much gratitude. But it is to Bob—husband, father, grandfather, best friend, chief cheerleader, and partner in this life I write about—I owe my deepest appreciation.

Faith Andrews Bedford

SECTION I
AS A CHILD

What a child doesn't receive, he can seldom give later.

P.D. JAMES

Sister Dresses

My sister's car disappeared over the top of the hill, her faint "toot" of farewell telling me she had turned onto the main road. The dust settled on our lane as I turned to the pile of boxes she left behind.

When mother died, Dad gave up the summerhouse.

"Come and take what you want, girls," he had said to us, and so we did.

I chose the tall secretary desk where Mother sat so often writing letters by a sunny window. Beth chose a painting of the summerhouse itself. Ellen picked a statue of horses, for she and Mother had shared a love of riding. After the moving van left with the things that Dad wanted, my sisters and I had lingered in the cottage going through drawers full of old letters, boxes of slides, albums of faded photos— the collective memory of a family. We had put it all into a dozen boxes, then each of us chose four. Beth dropped off my boxes first; Ellen's house was her next stop.

I sat down on the top step of the porch and opened a box marked "Albums." There were photographs of my father, resplendent in his naval uniform, and one of my mother leaning against their first car. Farther on was a faded picture of the family gathered for my christening, the women elegant in hats and gloves, the men's faces shadowed by their fedoras. As I slowly leaf through the pages, the family grows, we buy our first house, the cars get bigger. Then, there on the last page, is the picture of us in our sister dresses.

I could almost feel the starched ruffles and hear the rustle of the crinolines that were needed to keep the skirts nice and full. How well I remember Mother's delight when she found these dresses at the children's shop in the village. There was one in my size and one for Ellen but no size four for Beth. We were so excited when Mrs. Page, the shopkeeper, told us she felt sure she could order one for Beth that would come in time for Easter.

When the big box arrived in early April, we gathered around Mother while she lifted the dresses out, one by one. The pink tissue paper rustled as she held each one up. They were made of clouds of dotted Swiss—white organdy with blue, flocked dots. The skirt and collar were trimmed with tiny blue bows.

"To match your eyes," Mother had said.

We were allowed to try them on just once so that we could have a "fashion show" for Dad that evening. As we twirled into the dining room in our new finery, he burst into applause. Ellen and I daintily grasped the ruffled skirts and executed our best curtsies; Beth scrunched her dress up in her chubby little hands and made a close approximation of a bow, almost toppling over in the process. Then we had to carefully hang them up until Easter.

As I looked at the photograph, I could almost feel the pale April sunshine on our faces. We undoubtedly resisted putting on coats to go to church. They surely would have crushed those beautiful dresses and besides, then how could anyone see how wonderfully we matched?

In time, I handed my dress down to Ellen and she handed hers down to Beth. Finally, only Beth had one of those beautiful dresses, its bow a bit bedraggled after countless wearings by three little girls. But those dotted Swiss dresses were only the beginning of a long parade of matching sister outfits. Mother obviously was so pleased with the effect that she began an Easter tradition. I remember the year of the blue calicos and the year we all had matching yellow jumpers. Even Dad got into the spirit of things when he came back from a business trip to Arizona with Mexican dresses for each of his girls—even one for Mother.

Those wonderful white dresses, with rows and rows of bright ribbons edging the wide collars and hems, had skirts that were cut in a complete circle. Dad put Ravel's *Bolero* on the record player and we spun madly about the living room, our beribboned skirts fluttering like crazed butterflies. At last, we crashed, giggling, into a heap. Dad, quite pleased with our reaction to his gift, sat in his armchair and grinned his "that's-my-girls" smile.

As I looked at the photograph, I remembered those very first sister dresses so clearly that I am somewhat surprised that I cannot remember the last ones. Maybe Mother knew we were outgrowing the idea. Perhaps it was I who, at the sophisticated age of fourteen, first protested, saying something like "Really Mother, I'm much too old for that sort of thing."

Gradually, as we grew older, I think Mother saw how very different we all were becoming and just stopped buying us matching dresses.

By the time we were in our twenties, our lives were on three very distinct tracks. Our wardrobes clearly reflected our different worlds. I carried babies on my back; my clothes tended toward blue jeans and sweatshirts. Ellen was putting together outfits that could have been in the pages of *Vogue*. And Beth, a potter who actually went to the original Woodstock, favored bell-bottoms and Indian blouses.

Mother would shake her head in bemused bewilderment and say to Dad, "How did we get three such different daughters?" He would merely smile in response.

Though our lives have continued along different pathways, the circle draws closer as we grow older and once again realize how similar we are. Now we are all mothers and equally challenged by our various roles. Although our wardrobes are still very different, we all seem to be moving toward variations on "classic." Last Christmas, I gave all the women in the family silk blouses. Same style, different colors. Everyone loved them.

Mother didn't realize what a tradition she started. When my own daughters were little, I often made them sister dresses. When I was expecting my third child, I made myself a maternity dress out of some bright pink cotton. Eleanor, my older daughter, loved the fabric, so I made a jumper for her out of the scraps. That baby turned out to be a girl. So, in a way, my daughters' sister dresses started even before birth.

For as long as I can remember, Dad had always given Mother a beautiful nightgown each Christmas. They were long and silky, with plenty of lace. When we were little, we loved to stroke their satiny smoothness. With Mother gone, that tradition would stop. The first Christmas without her was bittersweet. The tree sparkled, but there was no big, pink box from "Sweet Dreams" beneath it.

We put on happy faces for the sake of our children, but all the little touches that Mother always added to Christmas were missing. Suddenly, Ellen drew out from behind the tree three identical white boxes. On the lids, written in Dad's bold hand, were the words "From the Nightie Gnome." We opened them and lifted out three identical red-flannel nightshirts.

We whooped with delight as we pulled them out of the tissue paper, then ran down the hall to put them on. When we came back into the living room to show off our sister nighties, Dad had put Ravel's *Bolero* on the stereo. We joined hands and did an impromptu dance. As the music grew louder, we twirled around faster and faster, ignoring the wide eyes of our disbelieving husbands and the gaping mouths of our children.

I smile now to think of the sight we must have made: Three grown women, dressed in red-flannel nighties, whirling madly through a jumble of empty boxes and wrapping paper. When the music ended in a clash of cymbals, we crashed, giggling, into a heap.

Our husbands shook their heads in wonder. The younger children nearly keeled over with embarrassment while the older ones held their sides with laughter. Dad just cracked his "that's-my-girls" grin.

Valentines in a Shoe Box

Our local grocery store is beginning to stock up on penny valentines. These tiny cards always make me remember the year our teacher announced that there would be a prize for the best Valentine's Day mailbox.

Excitement mounted as we gathered around the art table to pick out our supplies. Mrs. Taylor had laid out all the basics: red, pink, and white construction paper; colored foil; scissors; glue. There were some rolls of ribbon, the kind that curled when you ran the edge of a scissor along it, and even some jars of glitter.

Sharon Wilson asked if we could use things from home. When Mrs. Taylor said yes, competition shifted into high gear. Sharon, whose mother sewed, brought in real lace and some pink velvet. Ronnie Markham glued tiny white feathers to his box. They were from angel wings, he said, but I knew they were from his Dad's chickens; Mother bought a dozen eggs from Mr. Markham each week.

Five days before Valentine's Day, on my way to the art table for some more glue, I noticed that Dolores Kinney, who sat in the last desk in my row, wasn't working on a mailbox. She was making valentines, but I didn't see a box anywhere.

I liked Dolores; she was smart and always knew lots of new jump rope songs. But she never asked any of the girls in class over to play after school. She lived way out of town.

At recess I found her by the swings and asked her if she had finished her mailbox yet.

"No," she said, scuffing the ground with the toe of her worn shoe.

"Aren't you going to make one?" I asked, concerned about where we would put her valentines.

"No," she said quietly. "I can't."

"Why not?" I asked, mystified. She was the best artist in the class. Mrs. Taylor was always pinning her drawings to the bulletin boards.

" 'Cuz I don't have a shoe box," she replied in a heavy voice.

I was dumbstruck. Everyone had a shoe box or two.

"Did your Mom throw them all out?" I inquired.

"No," Dolores whispered, looking around to see if anyone else was listening. "Mother doesn't get our shoes in stores; she buys them at yard sales and church bazaars. They don't come in boxes."

I looked down at her sneakers. They had once been white but were now gray; one lace was knotted in the middle. I had noticed that Dolores's clothes were rarely new and her shoes were pretty scuffed and worn, but I thought that was because she had a big family and all her things were hand-me-downs.

On the bus ride home, I asked my little sister, Ellen, if she had noticed whether Dolores's brother was working on a mailbox yet. Joe sat right in front of Ellen in the second-grade classroom.

"No," she said with surprise. "He's not. I hadn't noticed it 'til you mentioned it."

When we got home, Ellen and I looked in our parents' closet for shoe boxes without any success.

"Mother," we said in unison when we found her in the kitchen. "We need two shoe boxes."

"But didn't I already give you each one?" she replied, looking confused.

"Yes," I said. "But I messed mine up."

"Me, too," said Ellen.

Mother gave us a long look and then reached up to the cupboard and got down the shoe box in which she kept recipes she clipped from magazines.

"You can have this one," she said, taking out the recipes and handing it to me.

"And Ellen, you can have the one Beth's new party shoes came in." Beth was our baby sister. The Stride Rite box was pretty small, but it would do.

Ellen and I hid the boxes in the bottom of our book bags. As soon as we got off the bus, we bypassed the playground games of hopscotch and dodge ball and went straight to our homerooms. I quickly lifted the lid of Dolores's desk and slipped the shoe box inside.

That afternoon, Mrs. Taylor announced, "I see that some of you still have work to do on your mailboxes. Since Valentine's Day is Monday, you may take your boxes home over the weekend and finish them up."

There were a few cheers and then a last-minute scramble for supplies from the art table. I saw Dolores pick out some shiny, white shelf paper and a little pot of glue.

On Valentine's Day, the classroom buzzed with excitement as everyone carefully placed their finished mailboxes on their desks. Mrs. Henderson walked slowly up and down the rows, a blue ribbon in her hand. She stopped, every now and then, to turn a box this way and that, or to bestow a compliment. When she got to the back of the room, she gave a little gasp. We all turned in our seats. Mrs. Henderson had stopped by Dolores's desk and was looking down in amazement.

"Dolores," she said, "however did you do this?"

Dolores looked down at her lap and blushed. "Eggshells," she said in a whisper.

"Excuse me?"

"I made it out of bits of dyed eggshells," Dolores repeated a little louder.

"Boys and girls," Mrs. Henderson said holding Dolores's box high. "I am sure you will agree that this box deserves the blue ribbon."

We all nodded in awe as we stared at the beautiful box. It was almost completely encrusted with dainty, pastel hearts and flowers made of what looked like tiny, mosaic tiles.

"How did you do that?" several voices asked at once.

Mrs. Taylor nodded her encouragement and motioned for Dolores to stand up.

"Well," Dolores began slowly, "I got the idea when Mother made scrambled eggs on Saturday morning. I remembered how, at Easter time, when we peeled our eggs, the colored bits of shell reminded me of mosaic tiles. Remember how we studied about the Greeks using them on their floors and stuff?" We all nodded.

"So," she continued. "I soaked the empty shells in food coloring for a while, then dried them and broke them into tiny bits. Then, I glued the bits of shell into these designs. My Dad sprayed the box with shellac when I was done to make it shiny and help keep the pieces of shell from falling off."

Mrs. Taylor began to applaud, and we all joined in. Dolores blushed and quickly slid back into her seat.

Later, as we passed out our valentines, a small crowd gathered around Dolores's desk for a better look at the blue-ribbon winner. We marveled that the leaves twisted and curled just like real ones do. Someone noted that the flowers had several shades of color in them. ("You just leave some shells in longer for a darker color," Dolores explained.)

After school, on our way to the bus, Dolores put her hand on my arm. "It was you, wasn't it?" I looked at the ground.

"You gave me the box, didn't you?" she persisted.

I nodded. "How'd you know?"

"Joe got a box in his desk, the same day I did," she replied. "Since your sister Ellen sits right in back of him, I figured you must have both given us boxes."

I smiled and asked, "Did he use eggshells, too?"

She giggled. "No, he said that looked too girly."

We both laughed, then she gave my arm a little squeeze and slipped something into my coat pocket.

When I got home, I pulled out a handmade valentine with a beautiful painting of an angel done in watercolors. She looked exactly like me.

I still save shoe boxes. You never know when you'll need one.

Be Mine

Children love to make their own valentines. Just supply them with plenty of construction paper, glue, glitter, paper doilies, ribbons, and lace and watch their imaginations soar. Make a fun card from a simple piece of construction paper, folded in quarters with "talking hearts"—the kind of candy hearts with little sayings on them—glued to the front and a special message written inside. Or, help your child make a heart-shaped valentine. Simply fold a piece of paper in half and draw a heart shape on it, being sure to leave several inches of the fold at one side of the heart as a spine. The ideas are limitless. Let your children's creativity be their guide.

Barefoot Summers

I hate shoes. I kick them off whenever I can. When my youngest granddaughter, Mason, was a toddler, she seemed to hate clothes as well, for she shed her garb at the least provocation. Me, I keep my clothes on, but I kick off my shoes whenever I can.

This morning, as we finish reading the newspaper, my husband's foot bumps into something under the breakfast table. He peers beneath it. "Three pairs of shoes!" Bob grins at me over his coffee cup. "That must be some sort of record."

" If God meant for us to wear shoes," I sniff, "we would have been born with them on our feet." But I sheepishly admit that three pairs extend beyond the bounds of acceptable untidiness.

I say I hate shoes because I can rarely find a comfortable pair, but the real reason I love the shoeless state is that it reminds me of summertime and freedom.

When I grew up in Illinois, we always kept our shoes on. It was one of Mother's unspoken rules. Inside the house, it was all right to shed them, but out of doors our feet were always safely confined in hot sneakers, Buster Brown oxfords, stiff patent leather Mary Janes, or sandals. During the summer, however, when we stayed with our grandparents on Cape Cod, shoes were optional.

Each August, we headed east, the summer sun turning our old blue station wagon into a sauna on wheels. After three days of driving, the fresh air rushing through the open windows finally bore the tangy sweetness of salt marsh. We turned off the sun-baked highway and slid into the cool tunnels of tree-shaded streets. My sisters and I knelt on the backseat to see which one of us could see The Little House first.

An old, weathered cottage that my grandparents bought as a summer home in the '50s to handle the overflow of visiting children and grandchildren, The Little House overlooked the tidal river that skirted their land. A sagging green and white awning shaded its porch. As we approached, we would crane our necks, trying to spot some cousins fishing off the jetty, their bare feet dangling over the high tide. We could feel our toes begin to tingle with the anticipation of freedom.

As we pulled into the driveway, our grandparents would be on the front stoop in an instant, waiting for hugs and tales of our trip. The minute we had dashed upstairs to claim our respective rooms (mine was the pink room with the Jenny Lind bed), we would kick off our sandals. It might be August, but for us, summer had finally begun.

By the time we arrived at my grandparents' summer home, our cousins had already been there for several months. Their feet were tough as old leather, and they could run across the gravel driveway with impunity while my sisters and I would gingerly pick our way across the stones, gasping at their sharpness. Though our feet toughened quickly, we would sometimes have to soak our throbbing feet in Epsom salts and water before going to bed. But we would never have dreamed of donning shoes to protect our battered toes. That was one of our own "rules of August"—from the first day until the last, my sisters and I did not put on shoes.

The only time I ever thought that shoes in August might possibly be acceptable was when I watched my cousins Susanne and Leila sashay off to the Friday-night square dances at the town boathouse. They looked so glamorous with their skirts held out by stiff crinolines, their hair sprayed into poufs. I could not wait to be old enough to go to the square dances, too. Peering at the festivities through the balcony railings (where children were allowed to watch), I decided I would even be willing to squeeze my feet into pointy-toed shoes to be able to whirl about on the smooth wooden floor as the caller shouted out "do-si-do."

The boathouse was a big, old barn of a building, weathered gray from a century of facing the salt spray that blew off Cape Cod Bay. Looking rather like a mother hen surrounded by her chicks, the boathouse perched above a small harbor dotted with sailboats. It was the site of an informal club devoted to teaching the town's children to sail and race small boats. I looked forward to the time when I could race, too, even though it meant putting on sneakers, necessary, Grandy admonished, to keep from stubbing a toe on a cleat or getting a splinter from the dock.

Decades later, I'm willing to put shoes on for those same summer reasons—to go to the store, to sail, and to dance—but the rest of the time I'm shoeless. In the winter, I pad around the house in woolen socks.

After breakfast, I gather up the shoes from under the table. The garden clogs and sandals are mine. The sneakers belong to my daughter. I smile as I realize I've raised another generation of shoe shuckers. I take the shoes into the bedroom and put them neatly away. That's where they really belong—in the closet, not on my feet.

THIS LITTLE PIGGY

Everyone loves sugar cookies. And most children love to go barefoot. Why not let your kids help you make a batch of "Barefoot Cookies?" Have them stand on a piece of sturdy cardboard, then trace around their feet and cut out two "foot" patterns. Next, whip up a batch of your favorite cookie dough, roll it out, and cut carefully around your patterns. With a spatula, gently transfer the dough "feet" to a greased cookie sheet. Bake as directed. When the cookies are cool, your children can decorate them. "Toes" can be polished in red sprinkles; sandals can be drawn in frosting. Encourage them to use their imaginations; then let them nibble away, one toe at a time.

Carving the Turkey

Thanksgiving at our house was always a festive affair when I was growing up. While Christmas was reserved for immediate family, Thanksgiving often brought to our table third cousins twice removed, bachelor friends of my father, recently widowed neighbors—anyone we knew who might not have already made plans about where to dine on that special day.

The meal required a full week of preparation. All the leaves had to be added to the dining room table, and sometimes a card table was placed at the very end. The linens were pressed and the silver polished. Aunt Gertrude sent her heirloom lace tablecloth out from her home in the city, and chairs were borrowed from any neighbors who could spare a few.

Mother was queen of the kitchen and marshaled her daughters like small troops in a grand plan of attack. A carefully prepared schedule was tacked to the kitchen door, and we began cooking three days in advance.

"No one," Mother said in true, Tom Sawyer fashion, "arranges a relish tray better than Ellen." And so it was that my younger sister welcomed a task that some might have considered an onerous chore as an opportunity to display her artistic talent. Ellen's tomato rosettes do her proud to this day. And I still marvel at Mother's ability to transform cooking tasks into opportunities for creativity.

Beth, the youngest of us, was often set to making the final flourishes, the little white paper ruffles that were placed on the ends of the turkey drumsticks. Her place cards, done in a childish hand with wonderful Pilgrim stick figures, lent bright dots of color to the snow-white tablecloth.

My job was to set the table. I took great care to make sure every knife, spoon, and fork was aligned straight and laid out at exactly the same distance both from the plates and from one another. One year,

I even checked out a book from the library on fancy ways to fold napkins. Startled guests and family were greeted at the table by something that was supposed to look like irises sprouting from the water glasses.

Guests always brought a little something to the dinner: a box of mints, a bouquet of flowers, a bottle of Port. We couldn't wait to see what the various hostess presents might be. We always hoped Mr. Meyers, an elderly cousin, would be to able join us for dinner, since he invariably showed up with a box of chocolate-covered cherries.

The most-awaited person of all was Grandmother. Sailing into the kitchen, she bore before her, like a proud figurehead, a tray with two pies: one mincemeat, the other pumpkin. Grandmother would carefully put her egg beater and a small metal bowl into the freezer compartment so, as she patiently explained, the well-chilled utensils would create high, firm peaks in her whipped cream.

The many Thanksgivings of my past stretch behind me like a long line of bright candles set on a shining table. There was the one in which we three sisters dressed up as Pilgrims, the one where my fiancé joined us for the fist time. But the Thanksgiving that remains foremost in my mind was the one when I discovered how honest praise could bring about miracles.

Guest and family had all gathered; grace had been said. The steaming turkey was placed before my father, the skin basted to a golden brown. As Dad pierced its glistening russet crust, fragrant juices ran down its sides and filled the well at one end of the platter. He carefully sliced thin slivers off the breast and began to stack them on one of Mother's best china plates.

"Don't you think you should save that for last, Jim?" Grandmother offered. "So that those breast slices will stay warm?"

My father looked up at her. "Probably a good idea, Mother," he replied, and began to spoon out the stuffing into the waiting bowl.

"You probably should hold off a bit on that too, dear," she suggested to her only child. "The warm stuffing will help keep the breast meat hot."

"Hmmm," Dad said noncommittally. He started to carve slices off the sides of the drumsticks.

Conversation began to flow about the table as the cranberry relish was passed and people complimented my mother on the beautiful turkey.

"Actually, Jim," said Grandmother. "It's a lot easier to carve the legs if you take both off whole and then slice them onto a side plate."

A small muscle at the side of Dad's mouth began to twitch.

"You know, Dad," I piped up in what I hoped was a helpful tone. "I think you're carving the turkey just right."

Dad's gaze, which had been fixed in fierce concentration on the turkey, now slowly swept past assembled family and friends to stop at me. The relish platter paused mid-pass.

The table grew silent.

"How much is your allowance, Faith?" he asked, pointing at me with the tip of the carving knife.

"Twenty-five cents," I said in a near whisper, sliding down in my chair.

"Excuse me?" my father said peering at me intently.

"Twenty-five cents a week, Dad," I repeated, forcing my voice through a throat constricted with apprehension.

Looking down the table at my mother, he said, "Joanie, as of today, her allowance is doubled."

"Done," said my mother.

I slumped in my chair with relief and looked at my mother and father. They were grinning at each other. Hesitantly, slowly, I raised my eyes to my Grandmother's.

She gave me a small smile, then turned to Dad.

"Excellent idea, Jim," she said.

Many Small Hands Make Light Work

Come the Thanksgiving Day feast, even the youngest children in your family can help out. Encourage little ones to make place cards, help set the table, and fold napkins. Older children can polish silver, peel carrots, and make celery sticks. Patiently demonstrate how best to perform each task, and remember to heap plenty of praise on children for their efforts and enthusiasm. You will all be able to give thanks for the many helping hands—and for the time spent together creating memories and traditions—during this holiday of gracious traditions and gratitude.

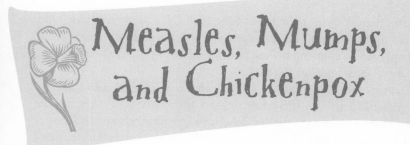

Measles, Mumps, and Chickenpox

Winter rain slides slowly down Sarah's bedroom window. She watches as the school bus stops at the end of our farm road, and she waves as her sister boards. It is the third day of a sick-enough-to-be-in-bed illness, and she's tired of her confinement. Turning her face away from the steam-fogged window, she asks, "Mommy, were you ever this sick when you were little?"

I smooth wisps of hair off her hot forehead and begin telling her stories of the years when childhood illnesses kept children home from school for weeks at a time. For me, mumps came first. The sight of my chipmunk face in the mirror made me laugh, but the pain of swallowing more than tiny sips of liquid brought tears. Meals were served to me on a little tray whose four legs folded down to make a table over my knees. Hand-painted leaves and flowers decorated the edges of the pale yellow tray that my grandmother had used for her children. Sometimes, next to my dinner of consommé and weak tea, a fresh flower would stand in a vase.

Mother made the trip to our village library twice a week and brought books home for me by the armload. When I was particularly feverish, she would read aloud to me, her soothing voice rising, then fading, as I drifted in and out of sleep. I loved to read everything from fairy tales to Nancy Drew mysteries and worked my way through every book on horses the library owned.

I had saved my allowance for months to buy three little model horses: a palomino mare, her colt, and a rearing black stallion. Then I turned my rumpled blankets into a miniature landscape. The plastic horses galloped over the high mountain made by my knees, wound their way through wrinkled foothills, and peacefully grazed in the smooth, flat expanse at the foot of the bed. On a card table that Dad had set up beside my bed, I made a stable for my horse family amid the paper dolls, coloring books, and the radio on which I listened to the *Lone Ranger* and *Roy Rogers*.

Measles followed mumps and Mother's arsenal of amusements was replenished. The little four-legged tray became an art studio where I turned clay into turtles, bowls, people, and, of course, horses. Paint-by-number kits filled my room with the heady smell of turpentine and linseed oil (only partially masking the all-pervading aromas of mustard plasters, Vicks Vapo-Rub, and eucalyptus oil.) Mother taught me to knit and to crochet. The card table soon became a jumble of knitting needles and balls of yarn, paintbrushes and cups of water, scissors, and crayons.

With measles came fevers so high that my room was darkened and my eyes were bandaged shut. Grandmother sent over dishes designed to tempt my almost nonexistent appetite: Floating Island, a delicate mound of meringue buoyed by a sea of lemon custard, and baked custard drizzled with maple syrup from the sugarhouse down the road. She and my parents frantically coaxed me to drink endless glasses of water after the doctor had mentioned the word *hospital*.

Lying in the darkened room, I made up stories that I intended to write and to illustrate with the watercolors I knew were somewhere on the card table. In the meantime, I learned to wiggle my ears and perfected my whistling.

When chicken pox appeared, Mother turned into an artist. To quell the terrible itching, she would paint my spots with calamine lotion and turned me into a tattooed lady or a clown. It was my responsibility to write down the total number of spots on a little notepad. When the count began to drop, she told me, I would soon be well.

Sarah hardly remembers her own bout with the chickenpox and, fortunately for her, measles and mumps are no longer a serious threat. As I help her sit up to drink orange juice mixed with ginger ale, she asks, "Is this one of Grandy's recipes?" Yes, I reply, recalling the many combinations of fruit juice and ginger ale Mother created to get me to drink the liquids so important to my recovery—concoctions made even more special by the addition of a straw.

My children have a special straw. It twirls and curls around and around, finally delivering juice to the thirsty patient. We use it only when someone is sick. As I set the glass back down on the table, I realize that, between my three children, I've only had to use this straw five times in the last sixteen years; modern medicine has certainly worked miracles. By the time Sarah has children of her own, perhaps even chicken pox may be a thing of the past.

Sarah has only been sick for two days; in two more, she will probably be well. Not for her the weeks in bed, darkened rooms, hot plasters on the chest. She reaches over for the little horse family and begins to trot the palomino mare and her colt down one knee and up the other. I reach for the black stallion and begin to gallop him across the quilt to meet them. When I was fourteen, I packed these little horses carefully away, figuring that someday I would be a mother and would need a way to amuse my children when they were sick.

"Mommy?" Sarah calls after me as I head downstairs to prepare her a lunch of consommé, rice pudding, and chamomile tea—a combination my mother discovered would tempt the appetite of even the sickest child. "This afternoon, can you bring up your scrap basket so we can make some blankets for the little horses?"

"Sure." I call back. Mother and I once created a little stable for my horses from an old shoe box. Perhaps Sarah and I will make one of those, too. Then I will teach her how to wiggle her ears.

Sweet Dreams

The queen was slim and elegant as she moved slowly among her attendants. I could not take my eyes off her. But Miss Henderson told us our time at the Nature Center was over; all fifth-graders had to return to school. I took one last look at the little bee-hive through its glass walls and reluctantly boarded the bus.

For the next three days I could think of little else. I pored through the encyclopedia's entry on bees and monopolized family conversation with dinnertime descriptions of the Center's observation hive and its fuzzy, yellow inhabitants. In an effort to satisfy my newfound enthusiasm, Dad agreed to take me back to the Nature Center the following Saturday.

I spent the morning with nose pressed to the glass, watching the nurse bees helping the babies out of their cells, the housekeeping bees carrying out bits of wax and debris, and the big, fat drones bumbling aimlessly around the hive. And, of course, I observed the queen. I was mesmerized by her stately progress across the face of the honeycomb. She paused briefly at each cell, laid a tiny egg, and then moved on.

Twice as large as the other bees, she had what appeared to be a beautiful jewel in the middle of her back. Actually, it looked as though someone had painted a green dot on her. I searched for the guide to ask her about the dot, but the volunteers were all outside.

That evening I got up the courage to ask if I could have a hive of my own. Mother arched her eyebrows and looked at Dad. "I don't think so," he said.

"But Mom," I pleaded, "you'd have a wonderful garden. The bees would really help with pollination."

She shook her head with finality and gave me The Look. I knew it was the end of the discussion. As if to soften their decision, Dad offered to take me back to the Center when the beekeeper, Mr. Miller, was there.

When that day finally arrived, I peppered Mr. Miller with questions while he was adding an extra box on the top of the hive. A "super," he called it.

"They've run out of room to store their honey," he patiently explained. "If they get too crowded, they'll swarm."

I nodded. Swarming, the encyclopedia had told me, was when some of the bees flew away to start a new hive.

"And what's that dot on the queen's back for?" I asked.

"Does it make her easier to see?" he asked me in turn. I nodded.

"That's one purpose," he explained. "The other reason is the dot tells me what year I put her in. Two years ago, the queen I introduced to the hive had a yellow dot on her thorax. One day, I could not find her and noticed another smaller queen with no dot. I knew then that the hive had become too crowded and the bees had raised themselves a new queen—the one without a dot."

"Where did the old queen go?" I asked.

"She left," Mr. Miller replied. "She took some of her subjects with her and swarmed."

"So after that the hive wasn't crowded anymore. Right?"

"Right," Mr. Miller said and returned to his work. I continued to think of things I wanted to know.

After he finished, he looked at me in amusement and told me I had too many questions for one man to answer. He led us to the bookshop.

"Here," he said, handing me a large book. "Read this, then come out to my farm and I'll show you the rest of my hives." I looked hopefully at Dad, who smiled in agreement.

A week later, Dad sat reading in a rocker on the farmhouse porch while Mr. Miller and I went through his hives. Dressed in his grandson's bee suit, I peered into the white boxes. Mr. Miller pointed out the bees going about their various tasks and showed me the "waggle dance" that they used to communicate. "It is a very organized society," he explained. "They have their own special rules."

I was enchanted. The hives were busy but orderly. Each bee seemed to have a job, and they all worked together in quiet harmony. A soft breeze blew the petals of the apple trees around us, and the air was full of tiny bees peacefully etching golden trails across a deep blue sky. I resolved that someday I, too, would be a keeper of bees.

That Christmas my parents gave me an ant farm, but it wasn't the same. I did term papers about communal insects and science fair projects about bees. I studied entomology in school, but nothing could take the place of having a hive of my own.

When he first met me, my husband found my interest in bees odd but endearing. He promised that, someday, we would have bees, but suggested that our first home, an apartment in New York City, was not an ideal spot. Little houses and little children kept my dream on a back shelf. Then, we bought some farmland in Virginia.

As we stood on the gentle rise overlooking the Blue Ridge Mountains, my husband put his arm around me. "We'll build a porch here," he said. "So we can have a place to watch the sunsets." Then he swept his hand toward a stand of persimmon trees and added, "And the beehives will go there."

That was twenty-four years ago. Since then, my gardens have been lush, my harvests bountiful, and I have all the honey my family and friends will ever need. In years when I have a bumper crop, I sell the extra in the village.

But harvesting nature's free sweets is only one of the reasons I love beekeeping. I regard my honeybees as tiny partners; together, we work in harmony as stewards of the land. I plant and weed and tend my gardens, and they pollinate my crops. Together we reap the harvest.

Now, as I sit on my back porch, watching my bees dart and swirl in the warm summer air, I remember the little girl I once was. I had many questions about bees then. I still do.

In an age when science has solved so many puzzles, when we can clone creatures and live for months in outer space, there are still mysteries. The behavior of bees is one of them. My books have plenty of answers, but there are always more questions

When winter snows drift across my hives, the bees gather into a little ball to keep each other warm. How do the bees in the cozy center know that it is their turn to move to the outside of the cluster and let their colder sisters have a turn in the middle? Why are some hives better at housekeeping than others? Even though I give my bees plenty of room, they sometimes swarm, and I can lose up to half of them in a blink of an eye. What can I do to prevent that?

But I do not mind not knowing all the answers. Living with Nature creates a sense of both wonder and humility. I will never solve all the mysteries. And that's all right.

The Plight of the Honeybee—And How You Can Help

America's crops are in danger. More than 30 percent of our fruits and vegetables (an estimated $5 billion worth each year) depend on honeybees for pollination, yet honeybee colonies have been decimated by the tracheal and varroa mites, parasites that infest beehives and against which the non-native honeybee has no natural defense mechanism. Especially hard hit have been feral honeybees—bees that have swarmed and set up camp away from human beekeepers.

Soon, only bees kept by beekeepers will be available to pollinate our crops and gardens. "Approximately a third of honeybee colonies in the United States have died in the past two years," explains Tom Seeley, a biology professor at Cornell University in Ithaca, New York. While no one can count the actual number of feral honeybee colonies, he estimates that this downsizing represents some 1 million colonies.

What can you do to foster honeybees in North America today? "Apart from becoming an active apiarist yourself," he says, "the best thing you can do for the honey bee is to buy more honey. On average today, American honey consumption is approximately a pound per person per year. If we double our consumption, there would be a greater economic incentive for professional beekeepers, which would translate into more bees to meet the increased demand."

Beekeepers are urging their congressmen and congresswomen to appropriate more money for research to fight the diseases and parasites that are crippling honeybees. You can, too.

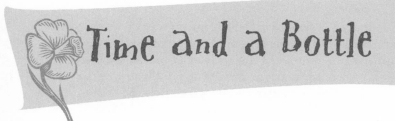

Time and a Bottle

A dozen pieces of sea glass march across the windowsill above my kitchen sink. They look like small sugar candies. One is pale green, and several are beige or brown. There are quite a few clear pieces; two are the color of lapis lazuli.

Once, these shards were hard and sharp—a danger to barefoot beachcombers. Perhaps some came from a jar thrown overboard by a careless boater. Others could be remnants of a bottle left lying in the sand after a picnic. Now, after years of tumbling about in the surf, the glass has mellowed, their colors faded—merely pretty reminders of a once-sharp brilliance.

As children, my sisters and I combed the beach for these bits of frosted color. Shells were everywhere, but sea glass was a treasure to be pounced upon eagerly. Our eyes became highly trained as we walked slowly near the water's edge, probing the drifts of small rocks and shells that the tides rearranged each day.

"There's one," Ellen would shout as she glimpsed a bit of green amidst the white shells.

"Oooohh, blue!" Beth would gasp when she spied that rarest of colors.

Sometimes the glass was still transparent and slightly sharp. It had not achieved perfect smoothness.

"Not done yet," we would declare if we found such a piece. "Throw it back."

And so we would fling the bit of glass as far out into the sea as our small arms were able, hoping that we might come again next summer and find it finished, worthy of adding to our collection.

Mother told us that long ago, in some fishing villages, people used to simply throw their trash into the harbor. From those watery middens, the fingers of the tide coaxed bits and pieces of glass and deposited them along the seacoast.

"Could our sea glass have come from anywhere?" we asked her.
She nodded. "And some of it might be quite old."

Mother had once told us that France lay on the other side of the ocean from where we made sandcastles on our broad stretch of beach. I looked out across the water and imagined that the misty white bit of glass in my hand had come from a perfume bottle thrown into the water a century ago by an elegant lady in Paris.

Sea glass comes in many different hues and colors. Green can range from bright chartreuse to dark gray-green—the color the sky sometimes takes on just before a storm. My sisters and I reasoned that these green bits must have come from ginger ale or maybe even French wine bottles. Pale aquamarine, we assumed, came from Coke bottles, and the brown bits, we were sure, came from our favorite soda pop—Orange Crush. But sea glass of pale amethyst and pink were mysteries. The rarest find of all was a piece of deep cobalt-blue sea glass. Such a treasure was easy to spot, for nothing in nature, not a shell, nor a rock, nor a bit of seaweed, possessed that astonishing sapphire color.

In the past, every time I went for a walk on a beach, I always found a piece of sea glass, sometimes several. This summer, for the first time in my life, I came back empty-handed. The environmentalist in me was pleased to see that people are no longer so careless with glass. The child in me was bitterly disappointed.

When my own children were small, I taught them the art of hunting for sea glass. "You need to walk slowly," I said holding their hands in mine. "Sweep your eyes back and forth across the drifts of shells and pebbles and, pretty soon, you will be able to spot the sea glass quickly."

But the children would race ahead of me. And I would laugh, realizing that asking a child to walk slowly is like trying to hold back an incoming tide.

And yet, they often did find the sea glass we so carefully sought. In time, they became expert beachcombers.

Over the years, we've collected jars full of the lovely stuff. My husband once made me a wind chime by hanging several shards of sea glass from a piece of driftwood. When we suspended it from a tree, it made a sound like the tinkling of ice cubes in a glass of cold lemonade.

But the pieces on my windowsill are the best of the best. One of my favorites is a piece of deep red glass frosted to a soft raspberry color. Another piece has been shaped by nature into a perfect pale green heart. And there are several tiny azure bits of sea glass, just the color of an August-blue sky.

How long does it take the ocean to turn a broken bottle into sea glass? A month? A few years? Decades?

Perhaps as long as it takes for a child to master the art of walking slowly. As I remember myself and my sisters racing down the beach in our hunt for the precious frosted glass, I see the three of us, our long braids flying out behind us. The waves whisper on the shore, tickling our toes; we laugh in delight as we try to avoid their reach. There is my mother standing tall, her hand shading her eyes against the brilliant sun as she watches us whirl about on the sand. Our bright bathing suits (green for me, red for Beth, blue for Ellen) help her distinguish us, one from the other. The demure skirt of her own suit ruffles gently in the warm sea breeze, and the gulls soar high above.

The currents of life have carried me far from those days. As I've tumbled about through the years, my own rough edges have, hopefully, grown smoother, too. The blond pigtails are gone. As nature frosts sea glass, so has she frosted my hair.

I rearrange the bits of glass on the windowsill and realize that I do not mourn the sharp glitter of youth. My life has acquired a certain soft patina. I've mellowed. Years of watching nature have brought an awareness of the constancy of change. I have gained an appreciation of the need to be flexible, having seen the fragility of things that are not.

I pick up a piece of creamy yellow glass, triangular in shape, and hold it in the hollow of my hand. I remember when I found this one. My sisters and I had never seen such a color. "Is it finished yet?" asked Beth. "Or does it need more time? Shall we throw it back?"

"No," I answered, putting it in my bucket. "It's perfect."

Silver Threads and Golden Needles

In the corner of my daughter's room is a little four-poster bed. On it lies my favorite doll, which I saved for my children to play with. She's covered with a tiny pink coverlet, edged in hand-tied fringe. The coverlet was my first sewing project, made when I was nine, from a snippet of a larger quilt my grandmother had sewn for herself.

As a little girl, I felt Grandmother could make anything in the world. When my favorite dress was badly torn (it really wasn't intended for climbing trees in, my mother observed), Grandmother rescued it with beautiful tucks and a clever pocket that hid the tear. If I admired a blouse in a magazine, its twin would appear a few weeks later, made even better with some pretty piping or special buttons. My dolls had wardrobes fit for princesses.

To a child, Grandmother's sewing box was a magic treasure chest: brightly colored spools arrayed in neat rows, scrollwork scissors in a tiny green leather case, glass-headed pins bristling on a red-cloth tomato from whose green-leaf top hung a little sawdust-filled strawberry for sharpening needles. Her thimble was too big even for my thumb. Lifting out the top tray by its satin ribbon handles, I would find lengths of lace, cards of colorful rickrack, and, best of all, the button box.

As Grandmother would stitch, I would sift through the buttons, sorting them by color or shape or size. There were sparkling rhinestone squares, little blue wooden buttons left over from a baby sweater, engraved pewter hearts, buttons of plastic and brass, and lots of mother-of-pearl buttons cut from shirts too worn to be rescued. Grandmother wasted nothing.

For my ninth birthday, Grandmother gave me a sewing box just like hers. I carefully pulled out the little drawers and discovered she'd lovingly filled them with spools of thread arranged by color, brand-new cards of snaps, papers of pins, a thimble just my size, and a beautiful button box filled with some of my favorites from her own collection.

In the 1950s, Home Ec was required for all girls. I still recall my first glimpse of that wonderful sewing room and its two neat rows of shiny black sewing machines with drawers full of mysterious metal attachments. My classmates and I learned to wind a bobbin, make a flat-felled seam, and master that most difficult of tasks—putting in a zipper.

Moving from potholders through aprons to gathered skirts, we began to plan our projects for the spring fashion show. A red calico shirtwaist was my crowning achievement. I even made my first attempt at custom couture: I added patch pockets and reduced the size of the collar. As I walked down the runway to the applause of family and friends, I saw Grandmother's proud face. She winked and gave me a thumbs up. Only she knew I'd ripped out the zipper three times.

When I was fourteen, my parents gave me a clothing allowance. I quickly realized I could buy one skirt or make three. The beautiful prom dresses in *Seventeen* could be re-created once Grandmother showed me how to adapt patterns. As my skills increased, I no longer suffered the frustration of designing a dress in my mind's eye and being unable to find it in a store; I could make it. I graduated from Simplicity patterns to Vogue. But, in racing to complete an outfit, I frequently made mistakes. One afternoon, finding me in tears over a totally ruined corduroy jumper, Grandmother encouraged me to learn the discipline of finishing a step or two at a time. The careful progression from cutting to marking to basting to finishing created an orderly pattern in my teenage life. Concentrating on the precise intricacies of fitting in a gusset or making bound buttonholes distracted me from such adolescent anxieties as biology tests, boyfriends, or drama tryouts.

My sewing skills progressed from prom dresses to business suits and, finally, a wedding dress. Grandmother helped me pack my home-sewn honeymoon wardrobe: a long skirt and a ruffled blouse for fireside wearing at our ski lodge, and a woolen cloak for the sleigh ride on New Year's Eve. She tucked in a lovely pair of new mittens that she had knit in a snowflake pattern.

When our first baby arrived, I learned to appliqué; little sailboats and trains decorated his sunsuits. The arrival of two daughters became an opportunity for embroidery and ruffles. During their naptimes, the discipline of sewing combined with the satisfaction of creating special clothes for my children made sewing my own brand of quiet therapy. I realized then, that my grandmother's gift to me had touched all realms of my life, for she helped me see the fulfillment in creativity that has extended far beyond needle and thread.

Grandmother has been gone for many years now, but her gift to me continues. As my children have grown and wanted things they could not find or afford, they too have discovered the creative pleasures of sewing. Drew, our rock-climbing son, recoiled from the expense of Lycra climbing pants and made his own. Our oldest daughter, Eleanor, brought home thrift-shop finds and altered them to become her own special creations. And Sarah has learned the knack of combining pattern pieces to create totally unique garments.

Now I have grandchildren of my own. As I work on their dresses and sunsuits, I realize these little garments are stitched together with the same thread Grandmother gave to me, the thread that binds generations together—the thread of love.

Pins and Needles

A small pincushion is an easy project for you and your child to make. Let your little one choose a bit of fabric and cut from it two squares, about 5" on each side. Now, pin the squares, right sides together and, with the shortest stitch on your sewing machine or using very small hand stitches, sew all around the square, leaving 2" open on one side. Through this opening, turn the square right side out and iron it flat. Fill the square with cotton balls or fiber fill, whipstitch the opening closed, and, voilà, you have a perfect little cushion for needles and pins.

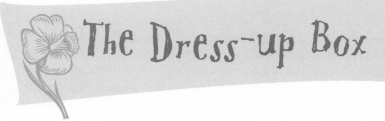

The Dress-up Box

I am the tailored type, most comfortable in well-worn denim or casual tweeds. My sister, Ellen, has been trying to update my look for years with little success.

A little while ago, when she became engaged, I told her I had nothing to wear to an evening wedding, so today she has volunteered to take me shopping.

At our first stop, she steers me away from a beige silk suit and pulls out several floaty things in colors like plum and teal. "Don't make a face like that," she says, pushing me toward the dressing room. " Just try them on."

I come out in the first outfit, a long chiffon skirt with an asymmetrical hem and a tunic top.

Ellen claps her hands and beams. "It's wonderful. The color looks great on you."

I shake my head no.

"It just needs some accessories," she says, ignoring my doubtful look and quickly heading off toward the jewelry counter.

"Now I know it isn't your basic black with pearls," she says, handing me some dangly silver earrings, "but just put these on and twirl around a bit."

I twirl.

"It's no good," I say in despair. "Every time I put on something like this, I feel like I've been playing in the dress-up box."

"Oh Lord," she laughs, collapsing into a nearby chair. "Remember the glamor?"

How could I possibly forget the treasures contained in the old steamer trunk? Into it, Mother tucked all of her cast-off finery: frilly slips and nighties dripping in lace, out-of-fashion high heels, pocket books with broken clasps, hats with veils. It became the repository for lengths of fabric, ballet costumes from our past recitals, and discarded curtains.

The bottom of the trunk held a cigar box full of costume jewelry. There were tarnished bangle bracelets that jingled wonderfully when one made imperious gestures (such as "Off with his head!"), fake pearls with peeling luster, and mismatched earrings. My grandmother contributed an ornate garnet necklace and pendant earrings. Her marcasite brooch was wonderful for holding capes together. My favorite was the long rope of iridescent Pop-It Pearls and matching earrings the size of silver dollars.

Grandmother's parasol, its lacy trim somewhat tattered, was prized by whichever of us chose to be the Southern Belle or Mary Poppins or My Fair Lady (Dad played that record constantly). Grandmother also contributed an evening bag beaded with seed pearls. It was in perfect condition but, she said, "I don't go to balls anymore, dears. You go for me." And so, in our dress-ups, we did.

Even the most mundane items had their place in the dress-up box. How could you properly play house without aprons and raincoats, bed jackets for sick people, and bibs for whoever was being the baby?

"Remember the midnight-blue satin?" Ellen asks, over lunch at a local café.

Mother had worn the long satin dress to her engagement party. We'd seen the pictures. She looked elegant in that wonderful gown from the '40s, with its pleated bodice, long skirt, and wide straps. Dad stood tall and proud alongside her, handsome in his naval uniform. By the time my youngest sister, Beth, was born, the satin dress had been relegated to the dress-up box. But we felt as beautiful wearing it as our mother had the night Dad gave her her diamond ring.

Dad contributed plenty of his things to the box, too: Dented fedoras, ties that had lost their shape, pin-striped vests, and his old Navy jacket. In them, I dreamed of being a fighter pilot, a lawyer, or a businessperson behind a broad, shiny desk like Dad's.

Aunt Gertrude's handmade lace tablecloth, no longer fit for the Thanksgiving dinner table, became a bridal veil in countless pretend weddings. It also made an elegant robe when I was a princess in our fifth-grade play about the Middle Ages. I made a hat out of a cone of poster board and taped a pink chiffon scarf to the point. As I gracefully glided onto the stage in the Oak School gymnasium, Mother and my sisters applauded the effect.

With a dress-up box, we could be whatever we imagined. If I felt hurt because I hadn't been invited to Linda Taylor's birthday party, I could be a princess who would never deign to mix with mere commoners. If Beth had a clumsy day, she could always put on an old ballet costume and glide about like a swan. The day Dickie Coleridge told Ellen to "grow up," she put on the midnight-blue satin, slipped her feet into some silver sling-backs that Ginger Rogers might have worn and, taking my suit-coated arm, went to dinner at the Ritz (milk and cookies at the kitchen table served by a haughty waiter...Mother, in an eyebrow-pencil mustache).

From our well-stocked dress-up box came all the props we needed to be doctors and mailmen, circus performers and cowgirls. We tried out various careers: grocery store owner, veterinarian (stuffed animals require checkups, too), and ship captains. Ellen was often a couturier and fashioned elegant outfits for her wealthy clients—Beth and me, our pocketbooks bulging with Monopoly money.

After a luncheon spent remembering our favorite costumes from the dress-up box, Ellen is eager to continue the search for the perfect dress. Two hours later, she's frustrated; I'm depressed.

"One more stop," she pleads as we approach a tiny boutique owned by the local seamstress. Marianna makes one-of-a-kind things, beautifully fashioned of exquisite materials.

In the window hangs a simple lace sheath. It is cream-colored with long sleeves.

"There," crows Ellen. "Isn't that just perfect? Simple lines; elegant fabric."

I hesitate and grumble, "It looks like Aunt Gertrude's tablecloth."

"You're impossible," Ellen mutters as she pushes me through the door of the shop.

She's right. The dress is perfect. I come out of the dressing room and turn slowly. She smiles and sighs. "You look just like a princess."

I look at myself in the mirror. Maybe not a medieval princess with a tall pointed hat but a princess nonetheless. A modern princess who wears blue jeans by day and lace at night.

I had forgotten the lessons of the dress-up box, that through clothing we can be whoever we wish, that make-believe can come true—if only for an evening.

Next week my husband and I are attending an anniversary party. A perfectly serviceable black silk cocktail dress is hanging in my closet. But suddenly I've grown tired of basic black. Maybe I should go as Mata Hari or Marlene Dietrich or Scarlett O'Hara. As I return to the changing room I spy, hanging on a hook, a shimmery green dress that sparkles with sequins. Perhaps I shall be a mermaid.

CREATE YOUR OWN DRESS-UP BOX

The magic and mystery of the dress-up are easy to re-create. And you don't have to look around for a box: The bottom drawer of a bureau will serve; a laundry basket on the floor of a closet works fine. Children don't care where it is; they love what's in it.

Look around your own closets and drawers for clothes and accessories you no longer wear—the brighter and frillier the better. Stop by thrift shops, the Salvation Army, and Goodwill, for instance, to see what they have on their racks. Lacy peignoirs and old high heels, fancy purses and hats with flowers are all wonderful in the eyes of children. But be sure to include both men's and women's items. Boys as well as girls can learn valuable lessons and find potential avenues of self-expression by imitating both male and female models.

Treasures can be found in unlikely places. Last week, I came upon a ballet school that was selling all of its old costumes in an effort to raise funds to send the students to master classes in New York City. I came away with pink tutus and a spangled, flame-dotted unitard with wings that must have been worn once upon a time in the performance of Igor Stravinsky's 1910 ballet, The Firebird.

Let your children help fill your dress-up box. They delight in finding props for make-believe; it is always interesting to see just what they choose. Ordinary items like old eyeglasses, rubber gloves, mismatched costume jewelry, and wayward umbrellas have a way of finding their places in "Lets Play Dress-ups." Tag sales, flea markets, and rummage sales also make wonderful sources for bits of finery and fantasy.

Let your imagination run free as you create the dress-up box. Think about your own childhood and the games you used to play. What costumes would you have liked back then? What roles did you play in make-believe?

Dress-ups aren't just reserved for little ones. By creating a dress-up box, you could recapture a bit of those times when you played grown-up and turn those memories into fun for your own children and grandchildren.

The Reading Chair

I t is a warm, sunshiny afternoon. As I read by the window, the sounds of children playing outside spark memories of long-ago summer days. Decades melt away and, for a moment, I think I hear my mother's voice calling my name.

As the sound of her voice comes closer, I quickly slip behind my father's ample, red leather chair. All afternoon, I have been nestled in it, reading. Now I have only fifty pages more until I've finished *The Black Stallion*. I know that if Mother finds me, she will make me go outside to play. "What are you doing inside on such a beautiful day?" she will ask. Then she'll tell me to run outdoors and find the other children. So I hide.

Father's red leather chair occupied a corner of his study, a large room filled with floor-to-ceiling bookcases. Beside the chair stood an old library table whose worn top supported a jumble of books, magazines, papers, pens, crayons, and games all gathered beneath a brass lamp with a leaded-glass shade. Beneath the table, my sisters and I piled the library books we brought home each week.

On the other side of the chair was a bookcase with three bottom shelves devoted to children's books. Some of these had been gifts to my parents; their musty pages and worn leather bindings testified to many readings. The inside cover of *Little Women* bore my grandmother's flowery script: "To Joan, Merry Christmas, 1932." Several volumes with wonderful illustrations, including *Treasure Island* and *Ivanhoe*, were inscribed: "To Jimmy on his birthday. From Father." Mixed in with these were my books: *Anne of Green Gables*, *Misty of Chincoteague*, the Bobbsey Twins' adventures, Nancy Drew mysteries, and fairy tales ranging from the Brothers Grimm to Hans Christian Andersen.

During the day, when Dad was at work, the red leather chair was my favorite place to be. I would curl up in it and read for hours, my legs dangling over its smooth arms. Since the chair was big enough to embrace two children, one of my little sisters would often join me in it, first choosing a book for me to read aloud and reminding me to "please do all the voices." Sometimes, Mother squeezed into Dad's chair with me. Scary stories were somehow better when she read them.

When Dad came home, though, the chair became his once more—and he filled it completely. After dinner, he would retire to his quiet corner, open his briefcase, and delve into work he had brought home from the office. Often, after we had had our baths, my sisters and I would run downstairs to kiss him good-night, only to find that he had fallen asleep over the newspaper, his long legs raised on a leather ottoman, his head supported by the chair's big red cushion. A mellow circle of lamplight shone on the bald spot on top of his head. We'd kiss him there and giggle as he snuffled awake.

Many mornings, my sisters and I would tumble over one another in a race to the red leather chair. We would pull up the cushion to see if any pennies, a dime, or perhaps a quarter had slipped from Dad's pockets, unnoticed, the night before. "Finders, keepers," Dad always said, but he made us promise to put the change in our piggy banks.

Each time our family moved to a new home, the chair moved with us, growing older and more worn ("more comfortable" said my father) with each journey. For a while, it stood in a corner of our basement playroom, but, after I left for school, Mother bought Dad a new, tweed-covered reading chair and put the old relic in the attic. I tried out the dapper new chair a few times. It wasn't the same.

When my husband and I bought our first home, we combed thrift shops, yard sales, and our families' attics and basements, looking for any cast-off furniture we might claim. Over by the window in my parents' attic, I spotted the red leather chair. I dusted it off, slid into it, reached over to a pile of old *National Geographic* magazines, took one off the top, and settled in for a good read. It felt like home; it was dusk before my husband found me. "You want that old thing?" he asked, eyeing the chair's scuffed legs and sagging seat. I nodded.

The red leather chair has moved with my own family several times. My husband has discovered that it is a welcoming chair, despite its age. The smooth, cool leather warms up after a few moments, and the supple cushions curve around each reader's special shape. Each year, on Dad's birthday, I give his chair a good cleaning with saddle soap, rubbing it until the mellow leather glows like a ruby.

When my children were small, their books were always stacked beside the red chair, which was relegated, by its faded elegance, to the family room or a study. With a bit of wriggling, one mother and two children could fit in it for bedtime stories. There I read *Heidi* to my children as I had to my little sisters twenty years earlier. I "did all the voices" for *Charlotte's Web* and wept all over again when I got to the part where Charlotte dies. When my children began to read, that was the chair they chose as their own. Curled up in it, they discovered the adventures of Laura and Mary Ingalls, the girls I met via the *Little House on the Prairie* books I carried home from my school's library so many years earlier. And, after the children were tucked into bed, the chair became my quiet retreat.

Now, with my children grown and gone, I have returned to school. To ease the commute, I've taken a small apartment near the campus and have furnished the tiny space with a few old things: a bed, a table and chairs, a desk, and the red leather chair. It is my reading chair once again, although the books I'm reading lately are a far cry from *Black Beauty* and not nearly as much fun as fairy tales. No Nancy Drew book ever had footnotes, and there was no need to highlight Dr. Seuss.

Years of reading and learning have penetrated this chair. In it, three generations have been transported to other times and other places. We have been introduced to new ideas, theories, and points of view. When I sink into its cushions and settle down for a few hours' reading, I become quickly absorbed; the pages fly by, and, once again, I lose track of time.

Now, as the evening light falls across my textbook and the children's laughter fades in the distance, I recall the times when I would hide behind this old red chair, not daring to breathe until Mother's footsteps had receded. Returning to my studies, I am content knowing that I may read as long as I like and no one is going to make me go play outside.

Passing the Plate

Our grocery store is beginning to fill with towers of pumpkin pie filling and displays of stuffing and cranberry sauce. Soon, the neighborhood children will be getting off the school bus, clutching tracings of their hands turned into paper turkeys. Phone conversations with our granddaughters are filled with excitement about their school's annual harvest dinner, complete with Pilgrim or Native American costumes for everyone. Our store has brown paper sacks filled with a Thanksgiving dinner for four that we can buy and then deposit in a box by the door for those who might not have a special holiday dinner—or any dinner at all.

A couple of weeks ago, I mentally began to calculate how many will gather around our own Thanksgiving table this year. When I opened the corner cupboard in the dining room, I was relieved to see that I had more than enough plates for everyone. Then my eye fell on the rooster china.

Several years ago, when my sisters and I helped Dad clean out the summer cottage after mother died, I came across the remnants of her kitchen china. I'd always loved its cheery motif of roosters, hens, and chickens. But over the years, as we children washed and dried the brightly painted dishes, the settings had dwindled. My own children's help with the dishes had further reduced the set to a few plates, a couple of serving pieces, and two cups and saucers. I rarely used them but could not bear to give them away. Yet the china was just taking up space in an already-crowded cupboard.

I pulled out the fat little teapot with the rooster crowing on its top. I'll keep this, I thought, and take the rest to the Salvation Army. As I wrapped the dishes in newsprint, I remembered the many family suppers that had been served on them. Perhaps, I thought, the china might brighten up someone else's kitchen and their children would have as much fun counting the roosters on the plates as I had. *May the meals served on this china be as delicious as Mother's,* I thought, as I put the last piece in a cardboard box. *May these gatherings nourish the soul as well as the body.*

Making sure that the homebound of our county have nutritious meals is the mission of Meals on Wheels. Volunteers take turns delivering a hot lunch and a box supper every day of the week. Today is my turn. We drivers are sometimes the only company our regular clients will have all day. For them, our visits are more than just food.

My route takes me through the oldest neighborhood in the heart of our small town, then loops out to a few cabins near the mountain and finally finishes up at a little cottage close to the village cemetery.

"Those folks there are my quietest neighbors," Miss Rose laughed when she first told me about when she and her husband, Henry, moved into the house after he returned from the war in 1945.

Like so many of my Meals on Wheels clients, it takes Miss Rose a while to answer my knock at the door, so I have plenty of time to admire her efforts to keep her tiny house tidy and trim. The last of the fall chrysanthemums are blooming in a circle around her mailbox. A faded American flag, much mended, snaps crisply in the cool autumn breeze.

Miss Rose opens the door and follows my gaze. "The Army gave that to me when Henry died," she says, smiling at the memory. "It was quite a surprise. Fellow just showed up at the house after the funeral. Said they do that to honor all the veterans. Pretty nice, don't you think?" I nod in agreement as I carry her meals through her little living room back to her kitchen.

Miss Rose does not like to eat her hot lunch from the aluminum tray that it comes in. She says it tastes much better if she puts it on a real plate. So, while I put her supper away in the refrigerator, she hooks her cane on the back of her chair and gets down a cup and saucer for her tea and a plate for her lunch.

When I turn around I see that instead of the usual blue dishes that always look so patriotic set on Miss Rose's red-and-white checked oilcloth, she has laid out a plate with a bright rooster painted in the center and a cup and saucer decorated with hens and chickens.

I catch my breath.

"Right pretty, aren't they?" she asks with a proud smile.

"Yes," I whisper. "Wherever did you find such lovely things?"

"My grandson, Travis, he took me into town last Saturday, and we stopped by the Salvation Army before we headed for home," Miss Rose explained. "I'd only stopped by to see if I could find me a top for my casserole there." She sweeps her hand toward a white dish sitting on her drain board. "Broke it last week when I was washing up."

I nod and she beams with delight. "But my eye lit on these pretty dishes, and I just wanted them so, I could almost taste it. They reminded me of when that old hen house out there was full of chickens. Henry and I made quite a bit of egg money from those old girls."

I look out the window at the little whitewashed building as Miss Rose continues, her voice softening. "Travis, he saw how much I liked the dishes and said he'd buy them for me for an early Christmas present."

Miss Rose begins to spoon her lunch onto the rooster plate. "Weren't many pieces left, you know. Only two cups and two plates. But that's enough for me and a visitor," she says, her eyes twinkling. "Won't you join me in a cup of tea and sit awhile?"

I am never able to spend as much time as I would like visiting with my clients since I must hurry along and deliver the lunches while they are still hot. Since Miss Rose is my last stop, however, I am sometimes able to spend a bit more time with her.

"I'd love to," I say, pulling up one of her white-painted kitchen chairs.

Some folks like to have me join them in saying a grace over their meal. Miss Rose is one of those. We hold hands in her little kitchen and say a blessing for food and shelter, children and grandchildren, good memories, and health to enjoy them all.

FINE CHINA

Children love to make their own "fine china." To make a fun plate for a special meal, just round up some plain white paper plates, a handful of crayons or markers, and turn your little Picasso loose to create a whole set of unique dinnerware.

Or, your children can turn their creations into special, permanent plates. Many toy stores have kits that turn children's drawings into unique plates. The kits contain special paper and washable markers. Once your little artist has created a design, send off the drawing and, in a few weeks, it is returned to you, turned into a beautiful, melamine plate. These make great gifts. Our own children loved making them for special occasions. One memorable Christmas, I received a plate with a wonderful drawing of a lopsided Christmas tree. "Mery Krismus, Momy, 1979" was written around the edge. And our grandchildren love eating from the "china" their parents made when they were little.

The Snowball

T he morning sun is shining with a winter paleness that barely warms the body and certainly does little for the soul. We're long overdue for a snowstorm; the tattered remnants of the last one have almost disappeared. There is nothing like a blanket of soft white upon the gray earth to lift my spirits and set the world to sparkling.

I scan the sky for clouds and see a few wisps rising above the horizon. These are cirrus clouds. In winter, they are a sure sign of snow. Pale at first, they grow steadily darker as evening approaches. I should go out and fill up the wood box.

As I put down my pen, my glance falls upon the little glass snow globe that rests on a stack of papers. When I pick it up and shake it, a ferocious blizzard obscures the miniature scene inside.

This little paperweight once belonged to my grandmother; it was one of her special treasures. When I was a child, she would let me hold it but only if I was sitting on the carpet and promised to be very careful.

Inside it is a Dutch village. The tiny china houses have angular, fanciful fronts, and a narrow canal runs between them. On the frozen water, little skaters glide: A couple waltzes elegantly, he in a tall hat, she in a fur-trimmed cloak. Four children chase each other, the little girls' pigtails stream permanently behind them as the boys forever reach out to throw snowballs. A chubby chimney sweep pulls his brushes on a sled. In front of him, a tiny dog frolics, but the sweep never trips over the puppy; the snowballs never fly. The Lilliputian figures are frozen in time and space.

The walk from our house to Grandmother's was only a few blocks long. We went through the village, up a hill, past the Thompson place, and into her yard. The Thompsons had three boys: Roger, Willie, and John. They almost matched my sisters and me in age. Just before Christmas, my sisters and I were on our way to Grandmother's house to help her string popcorn for her tree. We passed the Thompsons' house as Roger was pushing Willie on their tire swing. We called out, "Hi."

As Roger turned to wave, the swing arced forward, knocking him down and tumbling Willie from his perch. It made such a comic scene—Willie spinning heels over head, Roger's look of astonishment as the tire toppled him onto the lawn—that we began to laugh. But Roger had had the wind knocked out of him and lay choking in the last of the autumn's leaves. Willie began to cry. Beth, Ellen, and I stood transfixed in horror.

Suddenly, Roger's breath came back in great, sobbing gasps, and he began to cry, too. Then the boys looked up and saw us.

"Get out of here, jerks," Willie screamed. Roger stumbled to his feet, and the two boys began throwing acorns at us. We ran all the rest of the way to Grandmother's house.

We burst in the door, disheveled and short of breath. "My goodness," Grandmother said, looking at us in alarm. "You look like you've been chased by a tiger."

She sat us down with some cocoa and listened to our story. Beth began to giggle at the memory of Willie cartwheeling out of the swing, but Ellen remained frightened at the boys' anger. They were our friends. We swam on the same swim team in the summer; we played together at recess.

"I think your mistake was in laughing at them," Grandmother said, putting bowls of popcorn in front of us.

"But we couldn't help it," Beth said and began to giggle again.

"Probably not," Grandmother agreed. "But no one likes to be laughed at. Especially when they've made a mistake and, especially, if they are boys." She paused as she threaded a needle. "And, worse than that, you saw them cry."

"But everyone cries when they are hurt," protested Ellen.

"True," said Grandmother. "But boys think they're not supposed to. To cry and have a girl see them crying is, in their view, a truly terrible thing."

We shook our heads with what I realize now was probably the first in a long series of "why-boys-do-the-things-they-do" bewilderments and finished our cocoa. On our way home, we quickened our pace as we passed the Thompsons' house. The yard was empty. The cold, winter wind swirled dry leaves about the oak tree and spun the vacant swing.

On the playground the next day, Willie and John taunted Ellen and me, throwing their ball into the middle of our hopscotch game. And the following week, when we went to visit Grandmother again, they hid behind their bushes and jumped out at us just as we were passing, making us scream in fright. They rolled on the grass with delight at their prank.

Christmas vacation brought with it a wonderful snowfall, and by the time we returned to school, we hoped that the boys would have forgotten their anger, but the snow only gave them another weapon.

They kept a pile of snowballs ready and laid in wait for our weekly visits to Grandmother's house. We asked Mother if we could take another way, but she said no. The only other path took us by a lonely place, one without houses. It wasn't safe, she said.

We decided to fight back. Some of our friends made up a silly song about Willie, Roger, and John, and we sung it loudly on the playground. When they threw snowballs, we threw some right back. Once they caught Ellen and washed her face with snow. On that day, we arrived at Grandmother's house with Ellen, her face red and chapped, dripping with snow and tears.

"This has gone far enough," Grandmother declared.

"Are you going to call their mother?" Beth asked hopefully.

"No," she said. "You children need to work this out by yourselves."

We looked at each other, puzzled. How could we possibly do that?

She beckoned to Ellen, who was playing with the little snow globe. "Bring that to me, dear."

Ellen got up very carefully and placed the crystal globe in Grandmother's lap.

"These children look rather like you and the boys, don't they?" Grandmother asked.

"Exactly!" said Beth.

Grandmother shook the ball hard, and snow whirled fiercely. Inside the little ball, all was chaos. Then, slowly, the snowflakes settled to the bottom, and the village was calm once again.

"You see, I am in control of the storms inside this little paperweight. I can keep things wild and agitated all the time, or by just not doing anything, I can let everything simmer down." She paused and looked at us seriously. "You girls can do the same."

We looked at the children in the ball. The little figures remained still. The snow lay softly on the village scene. Everything was peaceful. Beth and Ellen and I glanced at each other. We wanted our friendship with the Thompson boys to be that way again, too.

You mean we should just do nothing?" asked Ellen.

Grandmother nodded. "You are in control of all your relationships. The decisions are yours."

"Do you think just ignoring the boys would stop them from teasing us?" I asked.

"Perhaps," Grandmother answered. "It would at least be a start. People usually tease others to get a reaction. If you show them that you are not going to pay any attention to them, they might stop."

So, on our way home, as we saw the boys lying in wait for us, we talked among ourselves and ignored them. We did not increase our pace. A snowball hit Ellen in the back, but we just kept walking. The next day at school, when John and Roger yelled that we were wimps, we paid no attention. The following day, when they began throwing snowballs at us on the playground, we just walked back inside.

On our next visit, we had to admit to Grandmother that our pacifist stance did not seem to be working. Frustrated by our lack of response, the boys only increased their teasing. I shook Grandmother's little snow globe and, as I watched the sparkling flakes whirl about, wished out loud for a return to the friendship we had had with Roger and Willie and John.

"Perhaps you are going to have to apologize," said Grandmother.

"What for?" said Ellen. "We didn't do anything."

"You laughed."

"But that's not bad," Ellen protested.

"To them, it obviously was," said Grandmother calmly.

We must have looked doubtful, for she added, "You cannot change other people, dears. You can only change yourselves."

"OK," I said, ready to do almost anything to remove the tension that existed between the boys and us. I looked at my sisters. "We'll do it."

Ellen started to object, but Beth put a hand on her arm. "Let's," she said. "I'm tired of the fighting."

After several cups of hot cocoa and a long game of Parcheesi, we got ready to leave. Winding our mufflers tightly around our faces, we set out for what seemed like the longest walk home ever. Sure enough, the boys were waiting for us. Roger stood up behind the bushes, arm poised to throw a snowball.

"Wait," I said, and put up my hand. He was so startled, he stopped his toss midswing.

"We're sorry we laughed at you and Willie," I said.

Roger's arm fell. His brothers' surprised faces popped up on the other side of the hedge. The six of us just stood there looking at each other.

Roger glanced back at his brothers. We saw Willie give a slight nod. "That's OK," said Roger. Then he grinned. "I guess Willie did look pretty funny flying out of the swing like that."

Beth started to giggle, but put her mittened hand over her mouth when I glared at her. This was serious business. One false move might mean a fresh barrage of snowballs.

"No," I said, affecting as much seriousness as I could muster. "We should not have laughed and we apologize."

"Right," said Ellen. Beth nodded vigorously.

Willie waved his hand as if to dismiss the whole event. Roger threw his snowball at the oak tree, where it landed with a satisfying smack.

"See ya," we said as we waved good-bye to the boys and walked on toward home. The boys waved until we were out of sight.

Grandmother left her paperweight to me. When I opened its box, I saw a note in her fine Spenserian script. It said simply, "For the peacemaker."

I look out the window. The snow has begun to obscure ordinary things. Familiar objects adopt their winter shapes. Where once there were beehives, there are now igloos. The birdbath begins to look a bit like a wedding cake. Soon the dead and desolate elements of the landscape will be united in a blanket of white. And, when the whirling snowflakes cease, a peaceful hush will prevail.

I shake my little snow globe once again and place it on the papers stacked on my desk. Grandmother was right; we can control whether our lives are stormy or tranquil. Inside my paperweight, the storm slowly subsides. The little village is peaceful once again, still and quiet in a soft embrace of snow.

Make a Snow Globe

Crafting your own snowy paperweight is a simple matter.

Choose a figurine or two. If you can find miniature trees or houses, you can create an entire village.

You'll also need: a glass jar with a tight-fitting lid (select a jar that's in proportion to the figures you're using), a small container of silver glitter, a hot-glue gun and glue sticks (not the low-melt kind), some water, and a tube of silicone caulking. For safety, kids will need an adult to use the glue gun.

Using the hot-glue gun, fasten the figurines into place on the inner side of the jar's lid. Allow to dry.

Sprinkle a good amount of glitter into the jar, and then fill it almost to the top with water. (Leave enough space for shaking.)

Run a generous bead of silicone caulking around the lid and screw it, with its glued figures, as tightly as you can back onto the jar. Allow the caulking to dry thoroughly. You can trim the jar's edge with ribbon or braid.

Turn your creation over, shake it gently, and watch it snow!

Paint By Numbers

The mailman toots as his truck rumbles up our lane. I wave from the garden, where I am putting in the last of the lettuce, and join him on the porch.

"Package from Utah," Henry grins, tapping the package's postmark. "Must be a valuable work of art."

I recognize my daughter-in-law's handwriting and smile. "You may be right." Jill often sends us our granddaughters' drawings. Henry likes to see them.

Quickly opening the package, I proudly pull out a portrait of my granddaughters. It is done in acrylics on canvas and signed by Jill. "Excellent likenesses," Henry observes. I agree; it's almost like a photograph.

Henry studies the painting and declares, "Looks like paint-by-numbers!" I nod; it has that unmistakable quality. "How did she do that?" he marvels.

"I don't know," I reply, shaking my head in amazement. "I'll have to find out."

I head inside to call Jill and thank her for this lovely surprise. Did she create this technique herself, I wonder. It wouldn't surprise me; she's wonderfully creative. But when I finally reach her, she laughs modestly and says that she found a place that turns photographs into paint-by-number kits and couldn't resist trying one.

As we chat, I recall the long hours I spent happily filling in the little numbered shapes outlined on the canvas: Red might be assigned the number 1, and all the areas marked 9 could be blue. Slowly, from a jumble of meaningless blobs, a painting would emerge: kittens, ballerinas, landscapes. My favorites were always horses. Mother discovered that the kits were a wonderful way to keep me occupied through endless bouts of measles, mumps, and chicken pox. After I hang up the phone, I decide to see if I can find the big box mother gave me when she and Dad moved into a smaller home.

The early spring sunshine filters dimly through the tiny attic window, illuminating the shadowy shapes of old furniture and dusty trunks. Behind the Christmas decorations, I find the carton that contains my childhood memories. Just as I'd hoped: There, beneath some letters from camp and my Girl Scout badge sash, is a paint-by-numbers canvas. Odd—I'd painted dozens, but Mother kept only this one. Holding it I am suddenly eight years old again, surrounded by the delicious odors of paint and turpentine. I am amazed that Mother let me paint in bed. But I was very careful. I would line up the tiny pots of paint on the card table she set next to my bed and thoroughly wash the small brushes in turpentine when I changed colors. Unlike Monet, who deftly blended the edges where colors met, I carefully followed the lines. My painted shapes sharply contrasted with one another. Nevertheless, when held at arm's length, the paintings were fairly convincing.

However, this canvas—a horse standing on a wind-blown hillside—looked rather odd. Instead of the usual blue sky sprinkled with fluffy, white clouds, the background was full of black thunderheads. The daisies in the field were black, too; patches of grass were brown.

As I puzzle over this strange picture, I suddenly remember what I had done. The stallion was supposed to be a palomino, but his mane was composed of shapes marked 17 (black) and 18 (brown). I knew horses: Palominos did not have black manes; they had white ones. Carefully cleaning my brush, I used 5 (white) and 7 (cream) to paint the horse's mane and tail. The painting looked perfect. But, when I went to paint the clouds and the daisies, I realized I was out of white. Mother found me sobbing into my pillow.

"What is it?" she'd gasped, wrapping me in her arms and feeling my forehead.

"I don't have any white left," I wept, pointing to where spaces marked 5 and 7 stood accusingly empty, "and I still have all these places to paint."

Mother frowned. "Didn't they give you enough white?"

"They did, but I used it all up on the mane and tail," I cried, "and now it's ruined."

Mother patted me gently until my tears stopped.

"You know," she said, holding the canvas at arm's length and studying it carefully. "The clouds might be quite dramatic in another color."

"Like what?"

" Well, what do you have left?" she asked.

"Black." I sniffed. "And a bit of brown"

"Perhaps you could pretend that a storm is brewing and the stallion has gone up on the ridge to make sure his mares are safe and do not stampede in their fright." The idea of such drama intrigued me.

"Think about it," Mother said as she tucked the covers in around me. "You know, artists can make their own rules." At the doorway, she turned and winked. "This might be a time when it would be more fun to be creative than to follow directions."

I picked up my brush and began to fill in the shapes marked 5 with paint No. 17. I created gray by adding black to the smidge of white left in one tub. I ignored the outlines. Dark, brooding clouds began to emerge. The whole effect was very striking. The black daisies looked pretty dramatic, too. Emboldened by my experiments, I decided the stallion's halter (light brown, No. 12) was rather ordinary. When the circus had come to town, the horses wore halters of purple and gold. Stealing a bit of the green intended for the grass, I gave my horse a colorful halter. The painting wasn't ruined after all. True, it did not look like the picture on the box, but I had made it my own. I signed it with a flourish.

I start to put my painting back in its box, then change my mind. Perhaps my granddaughters would like it. And if they ask me why the daisies are black and the clouds are not fluffy and white, I will tell them that life is not always painted by the numbers. Sometimes you need to follow your own inspiration.

May Baskets

Warm May sunshine floods my kitchen. Outside, the scent of early lilacs perfumes the air, and the bees are happily gathering nectar from the blossoms of the nearby orchard.

It is May Day, and the spring warmth has finally coaxed my gardens into bloom. As my children carefully tuck tiny, spring flowers into the bright paper baskets they will take to our neighbors, they beg me to tell them again the story of the years my sisters and I took May baskets to the witch.

Mrs. Pearson wasn't really a witch, but she lived on our lane in an old gray cottage with an overgrown yard enclosed by a sagging fence. Her gardens, Mother said, were once the envy of the neighborhood. Now, we rarely saw her. At Halloween, she would place a bowl of candy on her porch and hide behind her faded curtains. When carolers came to her door at Christmas, her house remained silent and dark. But every year, when my little sisters and I made May baskets, Mother would urge us to take one to Mrs. Pearson.

Our other neighbors always made a great fuss. "Look Arthur," Mrs. Peabody would call to her husband. "See what the fairies have left for us." Miss Addie Wilson, who lived in the house across the road, must have listened for our quick knock; sometimes, she almost caught us as we ran to hide behind her azaleas. But Mrs. Pearson never opened her door. Year after year, our little baskets hung on her doorknob until the daffodils dangled limply and the forsythia turned brown.

The year I turned ten, I begged Mother to let us pass by Mrs. Pearson's house. She just quietly shook her head. "You may not think so, but I know your baskets bring joy to that lonely old lady."

So, once again, Ellen and I, holding firmly to Beth's chubby little hand, crept up to her door, knocked rather half-heartedly, and scurried behind a lilac bush. "This is silly," I whispered to Ellen. "She never comes out."

"*Ssshhh,*" Ellen whispered fiercely, pointing toward the door as it slowly creaked open. A tiny, white-haired lady stepped onto the porch. She removed the May basket from her doorknob and sat down on the top step, our basket in her lap. Suddenly, she put her face in her hands.

"Oh dear, she's crying!" said Beth, darting out from behind the lilac. Mother had put Beth in our charge, so Ellen and I quickly climbed up the steps after her. We found her gently patting Mrs. Pearson's shoulder.

"Are you all right?" I asked with concern.

"Yes dear, I'm fine," she said as she looked up, wiping her cheek. "You don't know how much I love your little May baskets. I always leave them on the door so all the passersby can admire them." She paused and smiled shyly. "I just got a bit overwhelmed at the happy memories. You see, long ago, my sister and I used to make May baskets just like these."

Beth continued her patting.

"Would you girls like to come in and have some milk and graham crackers? I could show you pictures of when I was just about your age."

"Yes," declared Beth, marching through the open door. Since Mother had told us not to let her out of our sight, we followed.

As we sat in Mrs. Pearson's tidy parlor eating our graham crackers, she showed us old photographs of her and her sister rolling hoops down sunlit hillsides, playing with their dolls in the woods, and best of all, the two of them proudly holding their little paper May baskets trimmed with long ribbons.

I wish I could say that, after our visit, Mrs. Pearson began tending her garden again or that she answered the door at Halloween and admired our costumes, but she didn't. Nevertheless, for the next several years, until we grew too old to decorate paper baskets and hide behind lilac bushes, each May Day, we would climb the steps to her porch and find a little basket just for us. It was full of cookies cut in the shape of flowers. With pink frosting and sugar sprinkles.

A Maying We Will Go

The celebration of May Day dates back to ancient agricultural and fertility rites of spring. Many of the traditions for the first of May stem from the Roman Festival Floralia, a five-day festival that honored the goddess Flora with offerings of flowers, dancing, and ringing bells. Ancient Celts called their festival of spring Beltane, so named for Bel, the god of fire and light, both symbolic of a return to life, and of the defeat of the hard winter, with new hopes for good planting and rich harvests.

In many villages, a May Queen was chosen from the young, single women. The May Queen's job was to oversee the planting of the crops and rule the festivities of the day. She and her court would lead the May dances, the centerpiece of which would be the dance around the maypole. The maypole dance is traditionally a round dance of alternating male and female dancers, weaving in and out in a maze movement, plaiting ribbons as they go. In addition to pleasing the ancient gods of the harvest, the maypole dance also helped the young people of the village flirt and mingle socially.

The village children were sent out to the woods with baskets on May Day morning to gather the first blooms of spring with which to decorate the town and their homes. On the way home, some children probably left a basket on a doorknob or two and, from this, the tradition of leaving baskets of spring blooms arose.

Simple baskets are easy to create. Cut a 2.5-inch strip from an 8.5 by 11–inch piece of construction paper to create a square. Fold it in half from point to point and then in half again, so that you have created a triangle. Open the paper and snip away one triangle from one side of the square. Then fashion a cone from the remaining paper and staple on the strip as a handle. Paper or Styrofoam cups also make fine May baskets when decorated with bits of fabric, wallpaper, or tin foil and outfitted with a ribbon or pipe-cleaner handle.

Whatever you use as a basket, be sure to be lavish with your trimmings. Trailing ribbons, bits of lace, paper doilies, or glued-on artificial flowers can dress up even the simplest of paper cups. Finally, fill your creations with some flowers and hang them on your neighbors' doorknobs. Ring the doorbell and quickly hide in a place where you can be sure to see the look of delight on their faces when they discover what the May fairies have brought.

Lemonade and Independence

Today dawned cool and bright. It was one of those rare summer mornings when it seemed pleasant enough to bicycle to the village for the few things I needed there. By the time I finished my errands, however, the temperature had soared and the day was becoming sultry.

Pedaling back home beneath the blazing sun, I decide to take a slightly longer route, one that will take me through the old neighborhood where the streets are cool beneath the shade of mature maple trees. As I turn the corner, two little girls catch sight of me and begin to jump up and down in excitement shouting "Lemonade! Ice Cold Lemonade!"

Of course I stop; lemonade is just what I need. After quickly downing the first cup of cool, tangy lemonade, I slowly savor the second and admire the girls' stand.

They have taken great pains to make it pretty. An old card table is covered with a flowered sheet; a jar of wild daisies makes a charming centerpiece. Neatly stacked cups stand alongside a red and white ice bucket. A beautifully lettered sign reads LEMONADE. LARGE—25 CENTS. SMALL—10 CENTS. The whole effect is one of charming simplicity.

"How's business?" I ask as the younger girl, who tells me her name is Elisabeth, carefully counts out my change. Her sister, who introduces herself as Margaret, replies, "Not too good yet. You're only our third customer."

"But," chimes in Elizabeth, handing me two quarters, "it's going to be real hot today so I'm sure things will get better."

I tuck the coins in my pocket and smile at her optimism.

Watching the two little girls rearranging the flowers, straightening up the cups, and making sure everything is just right, I remember the lemonade stands my sisters and I used to have every Fourth of July. The town parade passed right in front of our house, and our stand was always wonderfully successful—especially when it was hot.

Preparations would begin days before as we painstakingly painted the sign that hung on the front of our table. Mother gave me an old muffin tin to use for change. I painted it white and decorated it with tiny red and blue flowers, carefully writing 1¢, 5¢, 10¢, and 25¢ by each cup. Dad gave me a cigar box for dollar bills, and I covered it with some blue and white–striped fabric left over from a pinafore Mother had made me. We mixed gallons of lemonade and emptied the ice cube trays into big bowls in the freezer so we would be sure to not run out on the Big Day. We wove red, white, and blue crepe paper through the wrought iron fence that bordered the lawn in front of our old, gray Victorian house and gathered flowers from Mother's garden for the table. The tall white snapdragons, frilly blue cornflowers, and sparkling red zinnias filled the house with clouds of fragrance as we carefully arranged them in a glass bowl.

The morning of the Fourth we rose early and put on the crisp white dresses that Mother had starched and ironed the night before. We ate our breakfast standing up so they wouldn't get wrinkled. Mother brushed our hair 'til it shone, then braided it, carefully tying it up in big red bows.

The parade always started at ten o'clock, but families began spreading out their blankets in front of our house long before then. We hurried to set up our stand by nine to be sure not to miss any early customers. Besides, our excitement could not be contained much past then. Placing our table between the two stone gateposts, we would cover it with the long white tablecloth that hid the extra cups and napkins we stored beneath it.

As the oldest, I was in charge of the muffin tin, carefully making change as the first customers began to trickle by. My sister Ellen filled the cups while Beth, the youngest, was the general maid of all things, running into the house for more lemonade, placing the ice cubes in the cups, or drumming up more business by running up and down the block calling "Lemonade at Number Eleven. Ice-cold lemonade."

When the sirens of the first fire engine heralded the beginning of the parade, we climbed up to the top of the gateposts to get a good view over the heads of the crowd that lined our street. Little brothers and sisters squealed with delight as they caught sight of their older siblings marching in the band. Sunlight sparkled off the tubas and trumpets and trombones; the drum majorettes threw their batons so high that they were lost from view by the leaves of the giant oak trees that lined our street. We waved to our friends as the Brownies and Girls Scouts filed by, and argued over which float was the best.

Business was usually slow as the parade went by, but as soon as the last marcher had filed past, we slid down from our perches and manned our posts. The biggest crowd came when the tired marchers returned from the parade's end at the fairground. Tired band members, with dusty uniforms thrown over their shoulders and instruments tucked under their arms, downed gallons of lemonade in five minutes flat. The Cub Scouts jostled for places in line. Costumed children, streamers dangling limply from the handles of their bikes, patiently waited their turns. By noon, as the last customers drifted back down the street, we broke down our stand, unwound the ribbons from the fence, and retreated to the shade of the porch, where Mother had laid out a special Fourth of July luncheon. We emptied the muffin tin out on the floor with a satisfying clatter and carefully divided the coins into three equal piles.

By our third year in business, Dad felt it was important for us to learn about the realities of the marketplace. Henceforth, he told us, we would have to buy our own cups and sugar, lemons, and napkins. When our piggy banks revealed little capital, he agreed to act as our bank and gave us a small business loan to be repaid on July fifth.

It was a sobering introduction to the world of business. As we went shopping with Mother, we carefully calculated just how much of each item we would need and diligently saved all the receipts. That year, as we counted our coins and paid Dad back, we learned the meaning of gross sales and net profits. Our shares were smaller than in years past, but we felt proud that they represented our true efforts and not merely our parents' largesse.

The following year another aspect of real business intruded—competition. The afternoon before the Fourth, as Ellen bicycled home from the village, she saw Tommy and Katie Miller (who lived two blocks down from our house) setting up a stand of their own. Dashing into the kitchen, she told us the dreadful news. We were horrified. That evening at the dinner table when we told Dad about the terrible development, he merely nodded and said, "Well, girls, looks like you've got competition."

"But what will we do?" we wailed, as visions of plummeting sales loomed before us.

"Just do a better job than Tommy and Katie do, and you'll be just fine," he said simply.

We stared at each other in confusion. How? Mother gently suggested that we make our stand as appealing as possible to attract attention. Ellen volunteered to make signs advertising our stand and post them all over the neighborhood. Beth offered to bike up and down the parade route handing out flyers.

As our excitement about our campaign mounted, Dad asked seriously, "And what about pricing?"

We looked at him not quite comprehending what he meant. "What are Tommy and Katie charging?" he asked Ellen. She thought a moment and replied, "Their sign looked like it said the same price as we always charge. Ten cents a glass."

"Well," Dad replied, "you ought to consider trying to beat that price."

Silence fell upon the table. Cut our price? Reduce our profits?

"How about . . ." I began slowly. "How about if we say 'Ten cents a glass. Two for fifteen cents'?"

My sisters eyed each other warily. Beth, who was just becoming proficient in math, protested. "But two glasses should be twenty cents!"

"Yes," I agreed, "but this way people will see they are getting a bargain and might buy more than usual." My sisters slowly nodded in agreement. Dad smiled.

That evening, in the pale light of dusk, we hurried about the neighborhood, tacking up Ellen's signs and gathering armloads of Queen Anne's lace to put in jugs perched on the gateposts. Dad said we could take the flag down from the porch and place it in front of our stand. Beth furiously hand-lettered stacks of flyers, declaring "Ice -

Cold Lemonade at Number 11 East Third. 10¢ a glass or 2 for 15¢."
We fell into bed exhausted.

Dad was right; we did just fine. Better than fine, actually. We made
more money that year than ever before. I'm not sure just what was the
magic ingredient. Perhaps the flag, snapping smartly in the morning
breeze, attracted attention. Maybe it was the flyers Beth handed out
so eagerly. Maybe it was our bargain price.

The following year we added homemade cookies and redoubled
our advertising efforts; we even took out a small ad in the local paper
(I talked the editor into giving us a special "kids' rate"). The year after
that, Katie and Tommy didn't even bother with a stand.

Today, remembering our years as budding entrepreneurs, I suddenly realize that I should not be surprised that each of us owns a
small business. Beth is a therapist in private practice, Ellen has an
accessory and clothing business, and I own a honey farm. I smile at
Margaret and Elisabeth, our neighborhood lemonade stand propri-
etors, and try to envision them in twenty years. Perhaps they, too, are
on the road to budding careers.

I become convinced of it when Margaret tells me earnestly, "Be
sure to come back next week. We're adding brownies." I nod and sug-
gest, "Perhaps a sign up by Main Street would attract customers. I
didn't really know you were here."

The girls' eyes light up, and Elisabeth claps her hands. "Neat idea."

As I wave good-bye and pedal homeward beneath the dappled
shadows of the tall maples, I pass a little boy pulling his sister in a
wagon. They are headed toward Margaret and Elisabeth's house. I can
hear the girls' voices faintly in the distance. Their words float gently in
the still summer air, a timeless children's chant: "Ice-cold lemonade
here. Get your ice-cold lemonade."

The Blue Pen

It has always seemed as though summer vacation was just getting into full swing when the back-to-school advertisements would begin to appear in our local newspaper. Suddenly, specials on American flags and suntan lotion gave way to ads for the local children's shop, bordered with little slates and pencils, apples and school bells. My sisters and I would spread out the paper and pick out our favorite outfits. I leaned toward kilts and kneesocks, Ellen liked anything with ruffles, and Beth liked plaids. Then, we would begin to gently pester Mother to take us to the village for a day of shopping.

"Goodness, girls," she would say in mock horror. "Didn't you just get out of school?"

By early August, as the Back-to-School banners started fluttering from the storefronts, she would begin to weaken as we stepped up our badgering. Finally, when a letter arrived with a list of supplies we would need for school, Mother would relent and help us make out our shopping lists.

The year I started seventh grade, a new school had been built. For the first time in our lives, my sisters and I would be riding a bus. We, who had always been "walkers" who came home for lunch, would now get to eat at school. Even the word *cafeteria* excited our imaginations. That year, lunch boxes topped my younger sisters' lists but not mine.

"Seventh-graders," I informed Mother, "do not carry lunch boxes; they use paper bags." She raised one eyebrow, but didn't argue as she led us off on our long-awaited shopping expedition.

Our Back-to-School day in the village was a well-ordered ritual. The first stop was always the stationer. Boxes of bright yellow pencils were piled neatly beside stacks of red, blue, and green spiral-bound notebooks; bins of erasers lay next to cartons of rulers. As Mother placed paper and notebooks in the cart, Beth and Ellen dashed off to find the perfect lunch box.

I lingered over the display of fountain pens. My grandmother had given me a beautiful one for Christmas the previous year. It was blue and my initials were engraved on the gold band at the bottom of the cap. "For my granddaughter, the author," she had written on the card. It was, Mother had told me, the kind of present you usually did not receive until you went to college. I treasured it.

Up until then, I had scratched out my writing in pencil. Now, aided by the pen's fluid motion, I filled entire notebooks with poems and essays, plays and stories. I experimented with different colored inks, carefully lowering my pen into the inkwell and pumping the little lever on the side until the pen was full. Peacock blue was my favorite color but black ink looked more professional, I decided. I tried out different signatures, practicing for the day when I would be asked to sign the books I would write. Everything I wrote with that wonderful pen suddenly seemed better.

The week after school had closed for the summer, I opened my pencil case to write a letter to my best friend who had gone off to camp. My blue pen was not inside it. I rushed back to my school and persuaded the janitor to let me into my old homeroom to look for it. The classroom seemed strange and desolate. The walls were stripped of all the usual maps and decorations, the blackboard was scrubbed clean, and all the chairs were piled on top of the desks. The principal even helped me go through the lost and found. But the pen had simply vanished.

I walked slowly home and collapsed at the kitchen table. "My pen is gone," I sobbed to Mother. "I'll never be able to write again." I knew better than to ask her to replace it. If Grandmother considered me old enough for such a pen, Mother had said when I first received it, then Grandmother also considered me old enough to bear the responsibility of taking care of it.

My shopping list said "pens," but, when I looked at the prices of the fountain pens, I knew I did not have enough in my piggy bank to buy one. Besides, nothing could ever replace the blue pen.

I dropped some ballpoints into my basket. Using them would be a sort of penance for my carelessness. I was sure my stories would never again be pinned to the "Story of the Week" bulletin board.

The shoe store was our next stop. Ellen had her heart set on patent leather, but Mother persuaded her to settle for black-and-white saddle shoes. Beth, tired of "sturdy browns," got sturdy reds, instead. I pleaded for penny loafers, and Mother, deciding that perhaps my feet were finally grown, relented.

The best part of a visit to the shoe store was when the salesman let us slide our feet into the X-ray machine to see if the shoes fit properly. We each took our turn to look down a little tube at our ghostly toe bones outlined by the shadow of the new shoe. When we wiggled our toes, the little ghost bones wiggled, too. I am horrified now as I remember the hours my sisters and I spent peering into that machine and laughing at our skeleton feet. But my toes are still firmly attached, so I assume all those X-rays did them no harm.

The clothing store was always saved for last, like frosting on a cake. Ellen headed straight for the party dresses, while I searched out the sweater sets. As the youngest, Beth received all our hand-me-downs. But Mother helped her choose one or two new things just for her.

It might have been August outside, but in the Patty Page Shoppe, we tried on sweaters and woolen skirts, parkas and knee socks. My favorite color was green, but Ellen despised it; Beth loved plaids, but I thought they were ugly. As the eldest, Mother told me, I had to be considerate of my sisters' needs and choose things that they would like after I had outgrown them. Votes were taken on my favorites. My sisters wheedled; arguments ensued; compromises were reached. Mother then carefully checked all our choices to see if our new wardrobes afforded the proper amount of "room to grow." Beneath the store's decorations of fake autumn leaves, we finished our shopping and reluctantly changed back into our shorts and T-shirts.

The next few weeks were spent putting up hems and deciding which new clothes we would wear on the first day of school. We packed up our book bags a whole week in advance. As I filled my pencil case, I felt a wave of sadness at starting the new year without my blue pen. I tried to tell myself that it didn't matter what I wrote with, but a heavy lump formed in my chest as I imagined a school year without it. I had written nothing all summer long.

When the big morning arrived it was, of course, seventy-six degrees outside. Mother tried to steer us away from wool, but we would not be dissuaded. Everyone, we declared to Mother, would be wearing their new clothes, and so would we.

Waiting for the bus, I sweltered in my green jumper and matching kneesocks. Beth wilted beneath her Shetland sweater. Only Ellen was comfortable in her blue cotton dress. She hated wool anyway; she said it made her itchy.

The school bus pulled up, and we hurried on, overwhelmed by the smell of new vinyl seats. We were thrilled to be "bus children" at last. Although Mother had driven us by the new Oak School as it neared completion, nothing could have prepared us for the impressive sight of the sparkling brick building with its vast, treeless playground. The halls smelled of fresh paint and echoed with the clanging of pristine metal lockers and the babble of confused children trying to find their way in an exciting new world. The bright September air seemed to bring with it the sweet promise of fall, when anything seems possible.

Mrs. Henderson was going to be my teacher. She had taught my best friend's brother two years ago, and he said she was "cool." When I found my homeroom, I realized that, amidst all the newness, there was much that was the same. The books on the shelves were far from current; the maps that pulled down in front of the blackboard were yellowed and cracked. On my desk, Danny Jordan had carved his name. He lived down the street from us and had been in college for two years.

I lifted the lid of my desk to tuck my notebooks inside and there, gleaming in the dusky interior, was my pen! Its golden band shone against the ink-blackened wood of the pencil tray. I caught my breath and quickly looked around the room. A faint smile crossed Mrs. Henderson's face, then she called us to order.

As the first strains of "The Star Spangled Banner" sounded over the intercom, we turned to face the flag for the Pledge of Allegiance. I felt myself slip into a familiar pattern, one that generations of American children had repeated before me and generations have repeated since.

When I became a mother, I always felt a sense of nostalgia as I watched my childrens' eager anticipation reach a crescendo on Labor Day. They worried about what teachers they would have and who would be in their homeroom. They carefully planned that all-important, first-day-of-school outfit and searched for last year's lunch boxes. Invariably, they couldn't sleep the night before.

When the old yellow school bus came rumbling down the hill to our house, my children tumbled into it, amid shouts of greeting from friends they'd not seen since June. And then, in an instant, they were gone, off to experience that wonderful newness and blessed sameness that the first day of school always brings.

I've opened the windows in the house this morning, and I can hear the school bus climbing our hill. It's been a while since my own children waited eagerly for its arrival, but I still remember their excitement—and my own.

This is a perfect morning to write each of them. On my desk is a fresh pad of paper and, of course, my blue pen. I pick it up, and the words flow smoothly.

"Happy first day of school," I begin. "May the new year be full of good surprises."

The Perfect Pencil Case

The perfect pencil case must be large enough to hold a ruler and a whole clutch of pencils and pens—and it should be made out of material of your child's choice, whether it's paisley-patterned velour, bright vinyl, or plain denim. Making a simple cloth pencil case is an easy sewing project.

Let your child decide how big the case should be and then buy twice that amount of fabric and a zipper the same length as the desired case. If your child wants a case that is, say, 13 inches long by 5 inches wide, cut two pieces of fabric that are two inches wider and one inch longer.

Lay the zipper, tab side up, on your work surface. Place one long side of each piece of fabric (right side up) on each side of the zipper, aligning the zipper tape in the center. Fold a half inch of the fabric under and pin the folded edges to the zipper, very close to the teeth. Using strong thread, stitch (either by hand or machine) the fabric to both sides of the zipper tape. Unzip the zipper a little bit.

Now position the two pieces of fabric so right sides are facing and pin the three sides of the rectangle together. Catching the ends of the zipper tape in the seam, stitch all the way around the case. Unzip the zipper and invert the case.

Optional: Should your child wish to keep his or her case in a three-ring notebook, make the pencil case an extra 1.5 inches wide and mark the locations of the three rings on the side opposite the zipper. Following the instructions on a grommet kit, install three grommets as marked.

The Memory Box

I had been looking for the perfect wedding present for my sister for weeks, with little success. I wanted to give her something meaningful and had just about given up hope when I went down to my laundry room to retrieve the picnic hamper. To get it down from a high shelf, I had to stand on a box in which I kept clothes that needed ironing. It was an old wooden box, battered and painted a dark green. It had been in the family for ages. Mother told me it was a sea chest and that its odd shape—slightly flared at the bottom—prevented it from tipping when the ship rolled with the waves.

Looking at it, I suddenly realized that I could refinish it. This sea chest would look perfect at the foot of the old four-poster Ellen had inherited from our parents. The two pieces would be reunited again, for, when we were growing up, the chest had always sat at the end of their bed.

I was the one who had painted the sea chest green. Before it became the repository for wrinkled clothes, the chest had served as our children's toy box. The children were supposed to put into it all the various playthings that didn't have a place on the shelves. Mostly it sat like an empty ship in the middle of a sea of LEGOs and stuffed animals, trucks, and blocks. Empty, it made a pirate boat or railroad car or a great hiding place for games of "Hide and Seek."

I didn't have much trouble getting off the green paint, but the next layer proved more difficult. It was a pale gold color, almost cream. My grandmother had sent the chest to my mother when we moved into our new house. I can remember watching Mother paint it to go with the English chintz she used in her bedroom. She'd made curtains and a dust ruffle of that lovely pale gold material strewn with roses of pink and wine and moss-green leaves and vines.

Mother must have done all this in a burst of nesting activity just before my youngest sister, Beth, was born, for I remember stepping on the chest to get up onto my parents' bed to see the new baby. In the middle of that great big bed, I was allowed to hold her. Sometimes, I just knelt on the chest and gazed in fascination at this tiny creature. When Mother lay Beth on her side, I would gaze into her deep blue eyes and wonder how soon it would be until she could play with me.

During its gold period, the chest was very important. When bad dreams woke me or thunderstorms crashed above our house in the middle of the night, I would run into my parents' room, leap up onto the chest, and then jump into their bed, where I would quickly snuggle between them—safe at last.

Once the creamy gold paint was removed, I discovered a deep-red hue. This must have been the color it was when my grandmother kept it in her house in Salem, Massachusetts, where I was born while my father was in the Pacific during the war. I thought of my Mother and Grandy dressed in the wide-shouldered dresses of the forties, hair pulled back from their faces in smooth, high rolls. Perhaps they sat together on the deep-red chest and listened to the radio as it crackled out the news each evening. It was a time of waiting. My father was an officer on a submarine tender; my mother's brother was on a destroyer in the Mediterranean. I wonder now whether they had sea chests of their own.

Grandy kept the winter woolens in the chest. The exotic, slightly medicinal scent of the camphor she used to keep moths at bay had seeped into the chest and filled its dark, quiet space.

My children were not the first ones to use the sea chest as a hiding spot. I can remember lying very still on top of the linens mother kept in the chest. The only light came in through the tiny keyhole. Suddenly the lid would be lifted, and a face would peer in at me. Sometimes, it was the person who was "it," and I would have to climb out of my fragrant hideout and take my turn as the "seeker." Other times, it would be someone looking for a hiding place.

"Go away," I would whisper urgently. "I got here first." Then I would put my hand up to help the lid close silently, so the thump of its closing would not give me away.

One rainy fall day, looking for a way to amuse my sisters, I suggested we build a fort. While they got out the card table, I went to my parents' room to find some sheets. As I lifted out the top layer of linens, I felt some lumpy objects. There, beneath the pillowcases, were three boxes wrapped in Christmas paper. One had my name on it. I gasped, then quickly looked about to see whether anyone had seen me discover my mother's secret hiding place. Gently and slowly, I closed the lid.

The deep-red paint was difficult to remove, but after much scraping—surprise—green again! And I thought I'd been so original. When the green would not come off despite solvents with fierce names like Red Devil and E-Z Strip, I began to despair of ever getting down to the bare wood. I stopped by the village hardware store and sought out Al, the solver of all household problems.

"How old is the chest?" Al asked.

I had to do some quick figuring. I knew that the chest had belonged to my grandmother's great-grandparents, Sarah and Samuel Benson. Samuel had gone to sea at seventeen and was captain of his own ship at twenty-two. He had rounded both horns and brought back spices and teas, porcelain and silks from the Far East. If he was the chest's first owner, that would make it about 160 years old. But perhaps it had originally belonged to his wife's father, Captain John Prentiss. Maybe Captain John had actually given it to his daughter, Sarah, while she was engaged to Samuel.

Sometimes, old chests like these were passed down from father to daughter and were used as hope chests. Into these chests, young women put their dowries: quilts and linens, blankets and embroidered tablecloths—all the things a new bride would need to set up housekeeping. If the second owner were the wife or daughter of a seaman, the name "hope chest" would have been very appropriate. The long, arduous journeys that the New England clipper ships logged around the world were fraught with dangers. The families left at home had little to do but pray and hope for their seaman's return. If its first owner had, in fact, been John Prentiss, the old chest might be well over two hundred years old. Its rough-planed boards and hand-forged hinges bespoke great age.

"Two hundred years, eh?" said Al. "I'll bet that's milk paint on it. Darn hard to get off. Almost impossible."

Al sent me home with his surefire, foolproof, atomic-strength mixture and with warnings not to get a drop on myself. I slathered the stuff on the chest, laid a sheet of plastic over it, and let it fester overnight. In the morning, my putty knife slid easily beneath the old, green paint to reveal a dark heart pine mellowed with age to a deep honey color.

I thought of Captain John packing this chest for a long sea journey, one that would take him from his family for as long as three years. Over our mantel hangs a copy of a portrait that was done of him when his ship, the *Liza Mary*, put into Amsterdam for refitting. He looks properly serious, posed in a dark suit, his ruffled stock peeking over a polka-dot vest. Was the chest built for him, and did he admire the sheen of the new wood as he packed it with the ship's log and telescope, his heavy woolen trousers, and oil skins?

Careful not to destroy the chest's patina, I did not sand the wood, merely smoothed out a few rough spots with fine steel wool. Then I applied three coats of varnish, rubbing it in well between each coat, until the chest glowed like old silk. I soaked some rope in strong tea to give it the appearance of age and fastened loops of it through the holes in the wooden handles. I polished the brass hinges and locks until they gleamed like gold doubloons.

As I ran my hands over the chest, I smiled and wondered what Ellen would put in it. Would she, like our grandmother, fill it with woolens, or with linens as our mother had? I remember once finding Christmas presents hidden beneath a top layer of sheets. Would Ellen hide presents in the chest, too? How many more children would discover that this chest is an ideal hiding place? And, when they were grown, would they—as I do now—respond to the smell of camphor by feeling like they were eight years old again?

I opened the lid and swept out a few bits of dust. The faint scent of camphor still lingered. Then I closed the top, sealing in my memories. I had loved it and used it well. But now it was time to pass the chest along to my sister, to the beginning of another family and more generations to come.

A Box for Memories

Children are born collectors. Why not help them file their treasures in an orderly way? A few shoe boxes, a bit of fabric, adhesive-backed paper or wrapping paper, some glue, and some labels are all you need to create memory boxes for your children.

1. Center the box on the covering of your choice and fold the fabric or paper so that it reaches up the sides and overlaps about one inch inside the box. Carefully miter the corners and trim off excess.

2. Now, spread white household glue on the outside of the box, place the box on the trimmed fabric or paper, and smooth the covering up the sides and ends of the box and inside the upper edges. Do the same with the lid.

3. Decorate with ribbon or braid, buttons, lace, as you wish.

4. Let your child think of a good name for the collection and ask him or her to print the title on a label that can be glued to the end of the box. Several of these stack nicely on a shelf, and the label helps your child tell at a glance what is inside.

Summer in a Seashell

A bove my mantel is a painting of a little girl holding a whelk shell. As she holds it up to the light, the sun streams through, turning the smooth, inner surface into glowing pink satin. No matter what the season, the painting's sunlight fills my study with summer's brightness.

Looking at the painting, I remember the story of its creation. The little girl is posing for her father, a painter. Her arms grow heavy, her neck aches, and she longs to rest a bit. "El, El, look into the shell," her father murmurs, and she remembers what a privilege it is to pose for him, how sought after his paintings are. "Just a bit longer," he promises, "and then we'll stop for tea."

Eleanor was my grandmother, and the painting—one that her father could not bear to part with—has been handed down through the generations.

For as long as I can remember, the shell in the painting sat on my grandmother's desk. In the winter, when cold fog rolled in off the sea, she would hold it up to the lamp, and its rosy sheen would fill her with summer's warmth once again.

Grandy found it washed up on the rocky shore of the little island in Maine that was her family's summer home. She used to tell me how, when the morning's silvery mists had lifted, she and her sisters and brother would run across the open meadows with their kites, pick bouquets of wildflowers, or gather the wool left behind on bushes by the wild island sheep. The children would hunt for wild blackberries and watch birds with their father, who taught them the birds' names and all their many songs. After tea, the children often explored the wide beaches, looking for pirate treasure. It was on one of these adventures that Grandy found the shell, scoured smooth by the waves, bleached clean by the summer sun. As generations before her had done, she placed the shell to her ear and heard the sound of the sea.

By the time my mother was born, Grandy had left that island home and created a new summer place for her own children. They, too, spent hours beneath the bright sun, sailing in little dinghies, galloping their ponies across the marshes, and gathering shells on the broad white strand of beach that bordered Cape Cod Bay. In this new summer home, Grandy re-created much of what she had loved as a child. She seeded meadows with wildflowers, designed perennial borders, and planted blackberries. From the wide porch of her house, she could look out across the tidal river and see ospreys nesting in a tall pine tree.

When we grandchildren began arriving, she set aside a part of her garden for us, so we could know the joy of planting vegetables and flowers. How proud we were to place a plate of our radish harvest— ruby globes scrubbed shiny and clean—on a dinner table made brighter still with vases filled with our flowers.

She taught us the birds' calls and showed us how to tell the difference between a gull and a tern as they skittered about the edges of the waves on the beach—waves, she told us, that could have come all the way from France. And she let us listen to the ocean in her shell.

Each autumn, as my family and I returned to our Midwestern home, I ached for the sounds of the shore, the cry of the gulls wheeling overhead, the low mournful sound of the foghorn so deep I seemed to feel more than hear it. The tangy, sharp smell of the salt air and the sounds of the sea were replaced by the smoke of burning leaf piles. But I missed the rhythm of the tides and the wildness of the shore. Grandmother knew my yearning.

One year, shortly after Thanksgiving, the postman brought a large box mailed from Massachusetts. Mother hid it in that secret place she kept all boxes that arrived in December. On Christmas morning, I opened my Grandmother's present and saw, nestled in tissue paper, the delicate pink and white of her shell. I picked it up, held it to my ear, and there was the ocean, murmuring softly. Outside, snow was gently falling past the windows, but in the shell in my hand, waves lapped upon a summer shore.

This year, I have a granddaughter of my own. Her birth heralds the beginning of a new generation. The stories of the past will be repeated; the cycle of life begun anew. When she comes to visit, I shall hold the shell up to her ear, and she will hear the sound that has always drawn the women of our family to the ocean. It is the sound of her own heart.

SECTION II
AS A MOTHER

There are two lasting bequests we can give our children.
One is roots. The other is wings.

HODDING CARTER, JR.

Sounds of a Summerhouse

I t is twilight, and, sitting at my desk, I can hear the gentle squeak of the porch swing as my daughter pushes it. Three squeaks, then the sound of Eleanor's bare foot swishing across the worn, wooden floor. I make a mental note to put a drop of oil on the spot where the swing's chains hang from large, wrought-iron hooks.

No one quite remembers how long the swing has hung on the porch. My mother recalls begging her big brothers to push her on it. It probably squeaked then, too.

My grandparents bought this house in 1920, a few years shy of its one-hundredth birthday. It had been built by a sea captain on a low rise overlooking a tidal river. From his door, he could see his ship bobbing at anchor and, in the distance, Cape Cod Bay. Beyond lay the Atlantic and the trade routes to the Far East, where exotic cargoes were laid into the hold of his ship.

This town was once the capital of the ship-building industry in New England. But the harbor silted in, sails gave way to steam, and the once-bustling port became a quiet summer town. Now the only ships that lie at anchor are little racing dinghies and cruising boats.

Each summer, as temperatures soared in the Midwest, my family would flee the heat to spend a month here with my grandparents. For Mother, that was going home. For me, this house and this little village with its long strand of white beach was my Brigadoon, a bright, sun-lit world that existed, I was sure, only for the month of August. After Labor Day, I imagined that it disappeared into the autumn fogs that rolled in off the bay.

My grandparents are gone now; so are some of their children. But each year, the sounds of summer bring them back, bring back all the players who trod my summer's stage.

The screened porch was my grandparents' outdoor living room. After supper, the generations would gather together on the swing, or in the collection of old wicker and rattan chairs whose worn seats would crackle and creak alarmingly as we settled down for an evening of reading or cards or charades. Once, when my cousin Ned sat down too hard, the bottom of his chair gave way with a loud rip, leaving him with his fanny on the floor and his ankles at his ears.

Of the eight wicker chairs, only one is left. But I cannot settle into it and hear its creak without seeing Ned, now a dignified lawyer and father of four, bent like a paperclip. And I can still hear the aunts shushing us as we laughed at his predicament.

The porch had no electricity, so evening reading was done by the light of kerosene lamps and an old camping lantern that had to be pumped and pressurized. It produced a soft glow and a gentle hiss. Grandaddy would balance the old Victrola on the living room windowsill and play his favorite records: *Oklahoma, Victory at Sea, South Pacific*. The old 78 records hissed as if accompanying the lamp. The lamp is still there, rusted somewhat, its noisy light illuminating our evening's reading. My husband says it would be an easy matter to run an extension cord from the living room so we could have "real light." I've told him I'll think about it.

The Victrola still works, too; Grandaddy's records haven't warped. Now, when Enzio Pinza sings "Some Enchanted Evening," I can almost smell my grandfather's pipe.

In the mornings, as soon as the early mists had lifted, my grandmother would send me down to the garden to pick a basket of new peas. Afterward, we would sit together on the old swing and shell them. The gentle squeaking of the swing was accompanied by a soft *kerplink, kerplunk* as the peas fell into the cook pot. *Squeak, plink, creak, plunk*. When we had finished shelling the peas, I would take the empty pods down to the chicken house and throw them over the fence to the hens. Their broody, sleepy clucks turned into loud cackles when they saw me coming.

Tonight we had the first peas of the season for dinner. As I sat on the swing with my daughter this afternoon, shelling them into a pot, their *plinkity, plunk* brought back memories of the smell of fresh peas steaming on the massive kitchen stove.

Now the kitchen is my domain. My daughter Sarah sleeps in the room above. When she gets out of bed, a certain floorboard squeaks loudly, and I know I shall soon see her face at the bottom of the kitchen stairs with a quizzical "what's-for-breakfast" look.

This morning, as Uncle Benny was dropping off a basket of sweet corn from his garden, he heard the floorboard squeak. "You could fix that with a bit of talcum powder, you know," he said helpfully. I continued to stir the pancake batter.

"Just sprinkle some talc into the cracks on either side of the board and step on it a few times. Squeak'll disappear right away."

"I suppose so," I replied after a moment. But I don't really want to fix the board. Then how would I know when Sarah was up?

This house, The Big House, is the center of a small family compound. Fifty years ago, my uncles each built cottages near the tidal river that wound its way past our land; The Little House, near the bridge, was bought for my aunts' families. If all of my cousins were visiting at once, there could be as many as seventeen for games of Beckons Wanted or Kick the Can. Each house had a bell for calling in its children to supper. Uncle Benny rang a ship's bell, Uncle Ralph rattled a cowbell, and those of us who stayed at The Big House were called in by an old schoolbell. The Little House had a whistle that hung by the back door from a leather thong.

The beauty of this, I discovered when I became a mother myself, was that children cannot argue with a bell. There was nothing to do but put down your bat, your racquet, or your dolls, shout "Coming!" and run home.

Now I stand on the back porch ringing the school bell. As its clapper strikes, *ca-clang, ca-clang,* I see my grandmother's tall figure, her arm arcing with a graceful swing as she calls us in. Sometimes, she would let me help her, but the bell was so heavy that I needed two hands to lift it and could only coax out a weak clank or two before surrendering it up to her strong arm.

Next to what was still called the Victory Garden stood an old, dirt tennis court. A ball lobbed into the garden's lush greenness was considered lost, so thick were the plants with summer's abundance. Come fall, my uncles always found several faded balls nestled close to the pumpkins or winter squash.

The screen porch gave a perfect view of any tennis match in progress. And, if you saw one cousin drop out of a foursome, you could grab an old tennis racquet from the hall closet and run down to take his place. The pong of racquet and ball often punctuated the heavy quiet of warm summer days. You didn't have to look up to judge the intensity of a game; it could be heard. When the balls began to go *thwap, smash* and the volleys of sound seemed endless, you knew the game was getting close to set point.

The end of a game was announced when the sound of racquets and balls was replaced by the soft swishing of a wide broom being dragged up and down the court and the *wisk, wisk* of the line tapes being swept. It was a firm family rule: Losers swept the court after each game.

The tennis court is still there; only the net is new. The players have changed, but the cheering is the same. The previous generation of family champions is all but gone. Now their children are content to watch their children challenge one another.

This morning, a particularly ferocious game was being played. Shouts of "love, forty" and "deuce" wafted through the windows. Listening, I remembered the long matches between my mother and her sisters. I had always hoped that someday, I might win a game or two from Aunt Nancy.

Down by the river, my grandfather built a small pier for the children. When morning chores were done, it was one of my favorite spots to take a book. I could lie on the sun-warmed boards and read or doze, lulled by the river's sounds—the soft lapping of water against the pilings, the drowsy murmur of the breeze in the nearby pines. If I put my eye to a crack between the boards, I could see the mussels clinging tightly to the pilings beneath the surface of the shadowed water or watch the little periwinkles making slow progress on the shallow river bottom. Sometimes, a fish would leap, falling back into the water with a silvery splash whose ripples would set the marsh grasses to rustling.

My grandfather liked to fish from the dock; my son does, too. As I lie on my back with my eyes closed and listen to the soft whir of Drew's line and the plop of the sinker as it hits the water, I remember my grandfather patiently instructing me in the art of casting and how to thread a worm onto a hook. I tried very hard not to make squeamish faces. After all, just because I was a girl didn't mean I couldn't touch worms.

There was always a little boat tied to the dock; in it, we all learned how to row. It was frustrating at the beginning; the oars would leap out of the oarlocks. When one oar was in the water, the other invariably seemed to be out. At first, violent splashings were all I could accomplish. Then my grandfather sat me in his lap, his big hands clasped over mine while he showed me the rhythm of reaching forward, quietly dipping the oars in, and pulling steadily until a stroke had been completed. Soon, I was good enough to take my two younger sisters out for a ride up and down the river. With our little faces peeping out above our puffy, orange life jackets, we must have looked like three bright-colored marshmallows skimming across the surface of the water. *Creak* went the oarlocks as I reached forward, *splash* went the oars as they dipped into the water. Tiny droplets would sparkle in the sunlight as I pulled the oars up for another stroke. *Creak, sploosh, drip, drip; creak, sploosh, drip, drip.* To this day, I cannot hear oars meeting water without remembering my sense of mastery and accomplishment and seeing my grandfather's proud smile.

As we rowed, gulls cried high above us as they wheeled and turned. Sometimes, they would drop a clam down onto the pier from a great height, then daintily pick out the meat. *Crash, crack* and the gulls would screech in delight. "Messy birds," my grandfather would mutter, as he swept the debris off the sun-bleached boards.

My daughter Eleanor and I went clamming this afternoon. The tide was low in the river, and we gathered a whole bucketful in less than an hour. Now, after a dinner of corn and clams, fresh peas and rhubarb pie, we have all settled in for an evening of quiet pursuits. All except Sarah, who has gone out to join her cousins in a last bit of play before bedtime. A new generation has learned the old games.

The crickets have begun their night song and, down near the river's edge, the peepers sing harmony. The owl in the barn and the whippoorwill in the woods add their notes to the summer chorus. As the fireflies begin to fill the evening sky with the Morse code of their tiny lights, I hear a child's voice calling in the distance, "Beckons wanted."

I don't need to look up to know the blue dusk is full of furtive little figures, darting out from behind a bush to give the needed wave.

The movement in the leaves of the linden tree outside the window tells me that some of the children must be hiding in its branches. It is as good a hiding place now as it was thirty years ago when my sisters and I would set the leaves to rustling with our stifled giggles. Our older cousins would silence us with whispered threats of katydid shells down our shirts.

From the distance comes a low rumble of thunder; the air smells heavy with impending rain. A breeze begins to stir the curtains at the window, and the house makes familiar creakings as it settles in for a storm. Soon rain will course down the roof, and the little place by the chimney will begin to leak again. Slow drops will fall into the old bucket that has stood beside the hearth for decades. *Pit, plop, pit.* The drops will hit the tin, and I will hear again my grandmother's voice, saying "Ralph, we must get someone to look into that leak." And, from the past will come Grandaddy's quiet, noncommittal "*Mmmmmm.*"

Perhaps I should have that leak fixed. My husband says he thinks he can do it. But I will not ask him. The gentle sound of the *drip, drip* is as much a part of a summer rainstorm as the boom of thunder and the crackle of lightning. Besides, if I banished the leak, I might banish the voices.

From the living room, I hear the soft click of checkers as my husband and son take up their nightly game. On the porch, the sound of the swing grows quieter: *squeak, squeak, swish; squeak... squeak... swish.* As the swinging slows, I know Eleanor's drowsy head is settling back onto a pillow. I rise to fetch the oilcan, and then think better of it. I could fix the roof, quiet the squeaking floorboards, silence a hundred little noises. But I will not. The kerosene lantern will continue to hiss, the rain bucket will stay in place, for if the rattlings, the drips, and the creakings disappear, so might the memories.

I sit back down and take up my pen once more. I shall leave the swing as it is, I decide. Some sounds of summer should remain as they are.

Angels, Stars, and Cowboy Boots

The year our first child was born, I gave him a special Christmas tree ornament, a star of his very own. Over the years, I have given him ornaments that reminded me of him or marked an important milestone in his life. When his sisters arrived, they, too, received an ornament each year. Slowly, our family tree became laden with wonderful, one-of-a-kind decorations, rich with remembrance. As we gather each year to trim the tree, we unwrap these treasured ornaments, laughing and reminiscing about the meaning behind each little keepsake.

On the Christmas that our second child, Eleanor, was five, we had just had another daughter. That year, I found a wonderful angel holding the hand of a littler one. "This is you," I told Eleanor, "and the little one is Sarah, who is holding tight to your hand because you are going to be such a wonderful big sister."

Because the ornaments belonged to them, I have always allowed the children to unwrap their treasures and put them on the tree themselves, no matter how young they were. On occasion, these ornaments were used as toys and it shows. There is a feathered bird that is rather bald, a wooden train with no smokestack, and a felt gingerbread man whose buttons have disappeared. Things that are well loved often look that way.

Eleanor always laughs as she unwraps her little angels, who have been hung on the tree for twenty years, and remarks on a missing wing. "Was that an accident," she asks, "or a reflection on the fact that I have not always been angelic?"

She loves the crystal ballerina that I gave her the year she began ballet lessons. While the little dancer spins on her satin ribbon,

Eleanor recalls the difficult choice she once had to make between becoming a professional ballerina or going to college. She chose the latter and has never regretted it. Her senior year in college, one of her roommates, spoofing Eleanor's dread of spiders, made her a special "spider swapper"—a flyswatter mounted on the end of a six-foot pole. To commemorate that joke, I gave Eleanor a carved Miss Muffet with a tiny spider sitting beside her.

Our youngest, Sarah, was very attached to her teddy bear. Needless to say, bears abound in her ornament box—carved, china, stuffed. A sparkling, golden bicycle marks the achievement of having learned to ride a two-wheeler and a replica of an antique plane commemorates her first airplane ride. For her fifth birthday, she was given a kitten; that Christmas, I found a little ornament with a fuzzy kitten curled up in a tiny straw basket.

Each year, as Sarah carefully unwraps her ornaments, she fondly remembers our many trips together: the week in San Francisco, where I found her the little wooden cable car, for instance, or the visit to Hawaii, marked by the straw palm tree.

The year she went on an Outward Bound sailing course, I gave her a little boat to celebrate her surviving her "solo" three days alone on a desert island. Last year, she remarked, "I'm not unwrapping ornaments, I'm unwrapping memories."

Drew, our firstborn and an enthusiastic athlete, has a stuffed–felt soccer player and a wooden skier, a china tennis racquet, and a carved kayak. As a child, his charging about the house earned him the nickname Drew the Dragon. So, of course, his box holds an intricately embroidered Chinese dragon, as well as a green ceramic one from Mexico.

As his interests turned to writing, I found Drew a wonderful Victorian scribe intently bent over a desk, a quill pen in his hand. When he was in college, he climbed Half Dome Mountain in Yosemite. To celebrate that conquest, I gave him a little hiking boot from Germany.

Several years ago, Drew married and moved out West. As our first Christmas without him approached, I climbed the winding staircase to the attic to look for the box of decorations. I paused to look out the tiny garret window at the fields beyond. Snow was beginning to cover the stubble of the autumn harvest. It was clear that we would be having a white Christmas. Behind a crate marked WREATHS and next to the box containing the crèche, I found the carton marked CHILDREN'S ORNAMENTS. I opened it.

Drew's box was easy to spot; he'd drawn a big dragon on the top when he was eight. Taking off the lid, I unwrapped a few ornaments: the skiing polar bear he got for his tenth Christmas, the Indian explorer I gave him the year he became a Boy Scout. Then, I came across my favorite, the little pair of miniature cowboy boots I gave him the year his father brought him back a real pair from Montana. Drew had refused to wear any other shoes for eight months.

I rewrapped the little boots in tissue paper. Then, I carefully put everything back in the box and took it downstairs. In the warm kitchen, now fragrant with the armloads of evergreen boughs cut that morning, I wrapped up Drew's ornaments in brown paper and twine.

Long ago, when I gave my first baby his first ornament, I had decided that, when my children married and had homes of their own, I would give them their ornaments. It was time to send Drew his. The little box was the seed from which his own tree of ornaments would grow.

I walked into the village to post the package, imagining Drew's surprise upon receiving it. As snow fell on the path before me, I smiled at the thought of the pleasure he would have telling his wife about each ornament, its history, and its meaning.

Several Christmases ago, Drew's gift to us was the news that we would become grandparents in a few months' time. I realized with delight that there would be a new little person on my Christmas list; another generation of tree trimmers has begun.

A star was just the right first ornament for a first grandchild. Someday, when her father lifts her up to place it on the tree, he will tell her, "This is your very first ornament, given to you the year you were born." Then he'll point to his own little star twinkling on another branch and say, "And that one over there; that one was mine." Her eyes will grow wide with Christmas wonder. A tradition will continue.

Special Occasions

O ur friend Steve dropped by to borrow our truck last night and found us just finishing up dinner. My husband poured him a cup of coffee and he joined us at the table. Steve looked surprised as he sat down. "Do you have candles every night?" he asked. I nodded and smiled.

I remember that evening so long ago when I called the family to dinner only to have them stop in astonishment at the dining room door.

"Did I forget an important date?" asked Bob, warily eyeing the flowers and candles on the table.

"Is it somebody's birthday?" queried our son, Drew, as he sat down.

"Mommy, you look so pretty," Sarah said, noticing I'd exchanged my usual jeans for a dress. "Is somebody coming for dinner?"

"Well," I began trying to put my feelings into words. "It's autumn, the air is crisp, the asters are coating the meadow with a frosting of purple, we're all healthy, and life is good."

The children gave each other their "Mom's-gone-round-the-bend-again" look and dug into their meatloaf.

How could I explain to them my day spent helping my friend Linda? Linda's mother died three weeks ago. After the funeral, I'd offered to help her box up everything from her mother's house. I had done the same sad work a few years ago myself and knew how comforting it could be to have some company.

We started in the dining room. Linda sighed as she opened a drawer in the sideboard and pulled out a set of linen place mats and matching napkins, still in their original box.

"Mother bought these when she and Dad went to Ireland fifteen years ago," she said, running her fingers over the embroidery. "She never used them. Said they were for a special occasion."

When we opened the corner cupboard, Linda took down a set of crystal champagne flutes. "She never used these either," she said. "She bought them in Chicago and declared that we'd all get to toast Dad and her on their fiftieth anniversary. But Dad died shortly after their forty-eighth."

With her finger, she pinged the rim of one of the flutes, and we both listened to the clear tone. "They could have spent all those years drinking champagne together out of these lovely glasses instead of waiting for a day that would never be shared."

From her mother's closet upstairs, Linda pulled out a blue silk dress with rhinestone buttons. The price tag was still attached.

"Let me guess," I said. "For another special occasion?" Linda nodded sadly.

When I returned home that day, I caught up with some paperwork. My sister's birthday was in a few days, so I reached into the desk drawer where I keep greeting cards that I buy whenever I see a particularly appropriate one. As I leafed through them, I came across one that said "For the World's Most Wonderful Mother." I never had a chance to send it to her, but I still cannot bring myself to throw it away.

That night, as I looked at my family around the table, I realized how much I take the future for granted. "Some day we'll. . ." is often heard at our house. But what if I knew just how many somedays were left to me? How would I live my life?

Well, for starters, I decided I'd clean house less and play with the children more. I'd read a book instead of finishing some project I thought was so important. I'd take more walks and more vacations, ride my bike and play the recorder. Polish my French instead of the silver.

I'd bear in mind that perfect is the enemy of good enough. I'd watch more sunrises (I'm not a morning person, but I can change) and try a new recipe every week (well, maybe twice a month). I'd call old friends and write to my sisters more often. I'd use perfume every day. And I'd always light candles at the dinner table.

My thoughts were interrupted by Eleanor asking, "Are you going to get dressed up every night now?"

"I just might," I replied.

"So can I wear my pink dress tomorrow night?" she asked, eyes wide with excitement.

I started to say that her pink dress was just for parties and church. I thought of all that extra ironing. Then I caught myself and answered, "Of course you can."

"I think we should make a toast," my husband declared, raising his water goblet. The children giggled and lifted their glasses of milk high.

"To life. To being together. To special occasions," Bob said, meeting my eyes knowingly.

"I'll drink to that," I said, clinking my glass with everyone's in turn. "May they happen often."

And they have.

Thank You, Uncle Arthur

One of the nice things about having grown children is that I don't have to bug them about writing thank-you notes anymore.

When my three children were little, I voiced their gratitude for the gifts they received in a family letter. By the time they were three, they could draw a picture of their present and dictate a thank-you note that I would include with the drawing. But once they were in school, they wrote their own thank-yous—with much prodding.

In the days following Christmas, I would frequently ask, "Have you written to thank Grandy for the book yet?" or "What did you say to Aunt Dorothy about that sweater?"

I would be met with mumbles and shrugs, clear indications that the note had not been written. I grew weary of nagging. The children grew increasingly mother-deaf. It would have been easier to write the notes myself, I often thought.

One Christmas, overwhelmed by frustration, I declared that no one would be allowed to read a new book, play with a new toy, or wear a new outfit until the thank-you note for it had been mailed. But still the children procrastinated and grumbled.

"It takes too long," groaned Eleanor.

Something snapped.

"OK," I said. "Everyone, into the car."

"Where are we going?" Sarah asked in bewilderment.

"To buy a Christmas present," I said tersely.

"But it's after Christmas," she protested, putting on her coat.

"No arguing," I said, in a tone of voice that the children knew meant exactly that.

As the children piled into the car, I told them, "You're going to see just how much time those who care about you spend when they give you a present."

"We know," grumbled Drew, slumped in the back seat.

"You don't know," I said, handing him a pad of paper and a pencil. "Please mark down the time we left home."

When we reached the village, Drew noted our arrival time. The girls helped me select birthday presents for my sisters at the Smart Shoppe. Then we turned around and drove home.

Bursting free from the confines of the car, the children headed for the sleds they'd left at the top of the hill. "Not so fast," I said. "We are not finished yet."

"But we bought the presents," Eleanor said, her hands on her hips.

"We've got to wrap them," I said, beckoning the children inside. They slouched through the door and waited while I got out the gift-wrap box.

"Drew," I asked. "Did you jot down the time we got home?" He held up the pad and nodded. "OK, please time the girls while they wrap the presents."

I made the children some cocoa while they wrapped Ellen and Beth's scarves. Drew cut the ribbon and timed his sisters.

After they had finished tying up the bows, they looked at me expectantly. "Now what?" asked Sarah.

"How long did this all take?" I asked Drew.

He considered his notes and said, "It took us twenty-eight minutes to get to town and fifteen minutes to buy the presents. Then it was thiry-eight minutes to get back home 'cause we had to buy gas."

"And how long did it take us to wrap the boxes?" Eleanor asked.

"Each of you did one present in two minutes," Drew said, looking at his watch.

"And how many minutes will it take us to go back into town and mail these presents?" I asked.

"Fifty-six minutes, round trip," Drew figured. "If we don't need gas."

"But you forgot standing-in-line time," said Sarah, who had often been the one to help me mail our packages.

"Yes," I agreed. "And, at Christmas, that can be a long time." Our post office can only hold about ten people. Twelve, if two or three are children. Between Thanksgiving and Christmas, those at the end of the line might shiver outside in the cold.

"Okay," Drew said, refiguring his sum. "We probably need to add about fifteen minutes for mailing."

"So," I said, "what's the total time we would spend to give someone a present?"

Drew added up his figures. "Two hours and twenty-eight minutes," he answered, tapping his pencil on the pad.

I laid a piece of stationery, an envelope, and a pen beside everyone's cocoa cup.

"Now," I said. "Please write a thank-you note and be sure to mention the present by name and tell what fun you will have using it."

The children rolled their eyes. Silence reigned as they gathered their thoughts; soft pen scratchings and cocoa sipping followed.

"Done," said Eleanor licking her envelope and pressing it closed.

"Me too," echoed Sarah handing me her note.

"That took us three minutes," Drew said, sealing his letter.

"Is three minutes really too much to ask of you to thank someone for a thoughtful gift that may have taken them two and a half hours to choose and send to you?" I asked.

The children looked down at the table and shook their heads.

"It's a good idea to get in the habit now," I said. "In time you'll want to write thank-you notes for many things."

Drew groaned, "Like for what?"

"Like for dinners or lunches," I said. "Or weekends at someone's home, or the time someone takes to give you advice or help on college applications or careers."

"Careers?!" Drew gasped; his first career as the family lawn-mowing man was currently on seasonal hold.

"So," Eleanor asked, "what happens if you don't write someone a thank-you?"

"Practically speaking, they'll never know if the present arrived," I said. "But mostly, they might decide that you are thoughtless and ungrateful."

"And rude?" Eleanor added.

"And rude," I agreed. I looked at the children seriously. "And if you don't have three minutes to spend on them, they might decide they don't have time to spend on you."

Sarah thought for a minute and said, "And you won't get any more presents!" Her eyes grew wide with horror at the thought.

"Did you have to write thank-yous when you were a kid?" Drew asked.

"Absolutely."

"What did you say?" he asked. I could tell he was formulating the rest of his notes.

"I really don't recall," I answered. "It was a long time ago."

Then I remembered Uncle Arthur.

Uncle Arthur was my great-grandfather's youngest brother. I had never met him, yet every year he sent me a Christmas gift. He was blind and lived next door to his niece, Becca. Each Christmas, she sat down with him and wrote out a five-dollar check to each of his dozens of great- and great-great nieces and nephews. I always wrote and told him how I had spent the money.

When I went to school in New England, I finally had the chance to visit Uncle Arthur in his old house near Salem's harbor. I was fascinated by his ability to find his way around his warren of little rooms. Some had ceilings so low that he came close to bumping his head. He fixed us tea and, as we chatted, he told me that he had always enjoyed my notes.

"You remember them?" I asked in surprise. "You must get so many."

"Yes," he replied. "But I've saved some of my favorites." He waved toward a highboy by the window. "Would you get the packet of letters out of the top drawer?" he asked. "It's wrapped in ribbon."

I found the letters and brought them to him. He laughed. "Could you find yours and read it to me, please? I can't, you know."

I had almost forgotten his blindness and was glad he could not see my crimson face.

I quickly found my handwriting on one of the faded envelopes. Taking out the old letter, I read: "Dear Uncle Arthur, I am writing this to you as I sit under the hair dryer at the beauty salon. Tonight is the Holiday Ball at the high school, and I am spending your Christmas check having my hair done for the party. Thank you so very much. I know I'll have a wonderful time, in part because of your thoughtful gift. Love, Faith."

"And did you?" asked Uncle Arthur.

"Have a good time?" I asked.

He nodded.

I thought back to that wonderful evening so many years ago. "Definitely," I replied with a smile I wished he could see.

Sarah's tug at my sleeve pulled me back to the present. "What are you smiling at?" she asked.

I told the children about Uncle Arthur's gifts and my surprise and pleasure that he had kept my note. I told them I was glad I had written a note each year; they obviously meant a lot to him.

"And did you look beautiful?" asked Sarah.

"My date said he thought I did," I laughed.

"Who did you go to the ball with? What did you wear?" asked Eleanor, no doubt visions of Cinderella filling her head.

"I think I have a picture of that evening," I said, going over to the bookshelves and pulling down a rather battered scrapbook. I opened it to a picture of me standing in front of my parents' fireplace. I'm wearing a strapless, black-velvet evening dress, and my hair is arranged in an elaborate French twist held firm with plenty of hairspray. Beside me, a handsome young man beams as he hands me a corsage.

"But that's Daddy!" Eleanor exclaimed, looking at the picture with surprise.

I nodded and smiled. "You looked pretty," Sarah said.

"Thank you," I replied. "That's what Daddy said."

As the children settled down to finish the rest of their notes, I stroked the faded petals of the dried gardenia pasted next to the photograph.

This past Christmas, Bob and I celebrated our fortieth anniversary. Thank you, Uncle Arthur.

PICTURES SPEAK LOUDER THAN WORDS

Children are never too young to learn the art of writing a thank-you note. When they are small, you can take a picture of them enjoying their Hanukkah or Christmas or birthday gift and, when it is developed, say, "Here is you with the present that grandmother sent you. What would you like to tell her about it?" Let your little one dictate to you his or her thoughts and thank-yous as you jot them down on the back of the photograph. Or, glue the photograph to some construction paper and write the note below it.

By the time children are around three, they can have fun drawing a picture of the present or of themselves enjoying the present. They can dictate a story about the picture to you. Be prepared for some interesting thank-you messages. One friend told me that her four-year-old drew a picture of a tall door with a small square beneath it. "Dear Nanny," he said. "Thank you for the toy box. I am going to push it in front of my bedroom door so that Matthew cannot come in and get into my stuff."

By first grade, thank-you notes become a wonderful way for children to practice their handwriting. My mother saved all of my children's efforts, and it is fun to see how their childish printing evolved into adult script.

A thank-you note should, of course, include mention of the present itself. But encourage your children to be particular in the description of the present, such as what they plan to do with it or where they will wear it or why it is such fun. They should also include a sentence or two to say what else was special about the day. Such phrases as "I hope you had a happy Hanukkah, too" or "I wish you could have been at my party," make a note special.

Every year, my children would inevitably ask, "Can't we just call and thank them on the phone?" The answer was always "No." But, then again, I suppose it's better than nothing.

A Soaring of Hawks

We've come to that time of year when the daytime haze no longer obscures the mountains and the evenings have a bit of a nip to them. Neighborhood children wear light jackets as they wait for the school bus in the cool of the early morning. The reds and golds of autumn have just begun to touch the treetops. Sweater weather, Mother used to call these early October days. At our house, these are all sure signs that the hawks will soon be here.

As if on cue, a dark speck appears on the horizon. My husband lifts the binoculars off their hook and goes out to the porch to scan the skyline. By the time I've found a sweater, two more specks have joined the first.

"Hawks?" I ask.

"Can't tell," Bob says, lowering the glasses for a moment. "Too far away. Might be turkey vultures." The dark forms and swirling flight patterns of vultures and raptors are similar; it is easy to mistake them from a distance.

Living in the foothills of the Blue Ridge Mountains, we are often treated to the sight of a hawk spiraling above our meadow. There is a quick flutter of wings as it hovers above its prey. Suddenly the hawk plunges toward the earth, wings tucked close to its body, looking as though it will surely crash. Then, at the last instant, it reaches out its talons, secures the catch, and swoops upward.

There is an old, dead tree in the lower field on which hawks like to perch. When it was first struck by lightning, we thought about taking it down, but now we would not dream of doing so. On the topmost branch of this old snag, the hawks sit, quietly surveying the meadow below with imperial hauteur, as though it were a grand buffet table set especially for them. We love to watch them soaring and then diving toward earth in what looks like a kamikaze mission. Sometimes, they succeed in catching their prey; other times, they don't.

It was at just this time of year, long ago, that our son, Drew, first spotted an announcement in the paper headlined HAWK WATCH THIS SATURDAY. He read the details to us at the dinner table. "Come join the Nature Center at the Inn on the Mountain and help us count the hawks as they migrate. Bring a lunch and chairs. Drinks provided."

The morning of our first hawk watch dawned clear and sunny. The girls helped me make peanut butter and jelly sandwiches; Drew and Bob found our beach chairs. We bundled the kids into the car and set off to the top of the Blue Ridge. There was no missing the Nature Center group. Off in the corner of the inn's parking lot, an assortment of trucks and cars were gathered. Children darted among the lawn chairs set out on the asphalt; a few were flying kites. Sunlight glinted off dozens of upraised binoculars.

We carefully threaded our way through the parked cars and found a spot near the edge of the lot where we could spread our blanket on the grass. When we opened the car doors, the children tumbled out excitedly and ran to join some friends. The joyous hubbub quickly subsided whenever someone shouted "There's one!" Heads turned upward; necks craned for a better view.

The afternoon wore on, but few hawks were spotted. The children were beginning to get restless. As we headed back to the car, a man from the Nature Center called out, "Sorry for the poor showing. It's early in the season yet. Come back next week." We waved a noncommittal good-bye and headed down the mountain.

It wasn't what we'd expected. Somehow, watching for hawks in the middle of a sea of asphalt, surrounded by cars and aluminum beach chairs, was not the quiet commune with Nature we'd hoped for. We all decided that we wanted to do this again but we needed to find a better spot, somewhere quieter and higher and closer to the hawks.

The following Saturday, the children were eager to be off to the "secret spot" that Bob had researched as ideal for hawk watching. We'd have to do some hiking, he said, so Drew whipped up a batch of our favorite trail mix. The girls made little pillows from my scrap basket, for they had decided the best way to watch for hawks was flat on their backs. We loaded everyone into the station wagon and headed for the mountains.

Our old car skittered on the loose gravel as we headed up the Gap Road. Two centuries ago, settlers' buckboards had made their way up this slope as they headed west over the Great Blue Wall, as the mountains were sometimes called. *If they could make it up this peak in covered wagons, we could certainly do it in a station wagon,* I thought, as I looked nervously at the steep dirt road before us.

The spent seedpods of the mountain laurel stood out against the shiny green leaves. They grew tall as they struggled up beneath the towering oaks and sycamores in their search for sunlight. A small stream had escaped from its culvert and burbled across the road. The children cheered as we crossed it with a splash. The old road ended at a gate hung with a sign that told us we had reached the national park boundary.

We piled out of the car and, donning our backpacks, headed up the fire road toward the top of Pasture Mountain. A half hour later, the trees began to thin; those that remained were gnarled and twisted as they clung to the meager soil of the mountainside. At the top of the mountain, Eleanor found a large patch of soft moss. We spread out our blanket and began unpacking our sandwiches.

"Look!" shouted Drew as he pointed overhead. High above us, circling lazily on a thermal of warm air was a hawk. Behind it, two more beat their wings to join him.

"Wow," sighed Eleanor. "Three at once." By the time we finished lunch, we'd counted seven more.

The northwest wind, moving across the Shenandoah Valley, hits the mountains and rises up in invisible spirals. Glider pilots love these thermals and so, obviously, do hawks. All afternoon, a steady stream of hawks flew overhead: sharp-shinned and Coopers, red-tailed and broad-wing. The girls handed out the pillows, and we lay on the soft moss and counted the hawks.

The warm, October sun soon lulled the children to sleep. The last thing I remember hearing before I, too, began to doze was Sarah's sleepy voice murmuring "Twenty-seven, twenty-eight . . ."

I woke with a start when Bob gently nudged me and whispered "Look." The children were already awake and gazing in awe as high above us five hawks circled slowly. Several more joined them, and soon there were more than two dozen hawks spiraling together, dark against the brilliant autumn sky.

"What is that, Dad?" Drew asked as he stared at the amazing black funnel of birds.

"It's a kettle," Bob replied in a hushed tone, as though he feared the sound of speech might break the spell that seemed to bind the birds together.

More birds streamed down from the north and joined the kettle until it seemed as though there must have been 100 or more hawks all circling together in a graceful dance. Then, slowly, a few broke away. Gradually, the dark funnel of hawks began to dissolve until just a few were left. And then, they too were gone.

Quietly, without our bidding, the children began to gather up their things. We hiked down the mountain in silence as though discussing what we had just seen might ruin the magic of the moment. As we left the windswept openness of the knob and entered the scraggly forest, Sarah began to spin. "Look, Mom," she shouted with delight. "I'm a hawk!" Eleanor joined her, and they swirled around each other, laughing. Drew followed at a more dignified pace.

Bob took my hand and smiled at our girls running and spinning down the trail. "I guess it won't be too long before they fly off on their own, will it?"

My heart ached at the thought. But I realized that this was what our job as parents was all about: to raise our children up to have the strength to soar off alone.

The touch of Bob's arm brings me back to the present. "Now that one is definitely a hawk," he says, pointing at a circling bird and handing me the binoculars. "This weekend, let's go up to the mountains." I nod in happy agreement.

We've continued to return to that same mountaintop each autumn; only now it is just the two of us. As we climb the trail, I always remember the magical day we saw the kettle; we've never seen another one. As Bob predicted, our children have, indeed, all flown off. But they come back often. And they have all soared.

Drew's Trail Mix

Our son's specialty is making a high-energy snack for our many hikes. While his recipe is very flexible, the main ingredients are:

1 cup salted, dry-roasted peanuts

1 cup raisins

1 cup M&M chocolate candies

Just combine these in a bowl and spoon into small, individual plastic bags—one for each member of the family. You can be as creative as you like with this. Some tasty additions could be other dried fruits (dried banana and flaked coconut are particularly good) and little pretzels. Some people enjoy substituting Reese's Pieces or carob chips for the M&Ms.

The Honor Jar

The produce stand down at the crossroads has added "Silver Queen Corn" to the long list of fruits and vegetables for sale. That's always a sure sign that it's the peak of harvest season. As I wave to the farmer, I remember the year we always refer to as the "summer of the bumper crops."

Ample rain and mild weather kept the lettuce from bolting early and the tomatoes from scorching. For some reason, the squash beetles didn't appear, and the potato bugs fled from my hot-pepper spray, just as they were supposed to.

We had fresh vegetables at every meal, including breakfast. Zucchini was served fried, baked, stuffed, and hidden in meat loaf. Corn on the cob and sliced tomatoes, always family favorites, began to be met with groans.

I used up all my canning jars, the freezer was full to bursting, and the porch rafters were festooned with strings of sliced squash hanging to dry in the summer breeze. One evening, I sank wearily down at the dinner table and said, "The garden is overflowing."

"I suppose you've put up as much as you can," my husband said.

I smiled weakly and nodded.

"You could give some to the neighbors," he offered helpfully.

"I've done that," I sighed. "Caroline and Ruth almost hide now when they see me coming."

The children, who had been listening silently while gamely downing yet another meal of beans, began whispering among themselves.

"How about if we have a produce stand?" Drew asked.

"That's a good idea, dear," I said. "But I really don't have time to set one up."

"We'll do it," Drew offered.

"All by ourselves," Eleanor added.

I must have looked skeptical, for Sarah piped up, "That way you'll have much less to pick, Mom."

I laughed and looked at Bob. He grinned at the kids. "OK. It's all yours."

The next morning the children were out in the garden even before the morning mists had lifted. By eight, they'd turned my kitchen into a small battle station.

The girls polished tomatoes to a ruby glow while Drew carefully arranged zucchinis in an old enamel bowl. In the basement, Sarah found some green plastic berry baskets I'd been saving for a Christmas project. She filled them with exactly thirty green beans each. Finally satisfied, they loaded their harvest into Eleanor's wagon. Piled high with multicolored vegetables, the Red Flyer looked like a festive gypsy wagon.

To the mailbox, they tacked a brown paper bag on which Eleanor had written in bold letters, "Fresh Produce." Then, they sat down on a blanket in the shade of the big maples and waited for their first customer.

The combination of freshly scrubbed vegetables and three eager, expectant faces must have been irresistible. They sold out by ten o'clock.

As they spread the change out on the kitchen table, they enthusiastically plotted the next day's stand.

"Let's sell flowers, too," suggested Sarah, always my helper when it came to flower arrangements.

"Can we grub for some new potatoes, Mom?" Eleanor asked.

"As long as you leave the deep ones for the fall digging, sure."

By ten the next morning, the air was hot and sultry, and the wagon was still half full. At noon the kids came trudging up the lane with a few boxes of beans left.

"Looks like green beans for dinner tonight," I said. Sarah rolled her eyes and made a face.

At dinner they reported, "We sold almost everything, but lots of cars passed us by."

"Maybe you need a bigger stand to attract more attention," Bob said.

"Would that take money?" Eleanor asked looking concerned.

Bob laughed, "I've probably got enough scrap lumber in the barn."

That Saturday was filled with the sounds of hammering and sawing. By evening, the children's faces and hands were so covered with paint spatters that I felt as though I was serving dinner to a tribe of warriors. Bob confessed to amazement at how three children could use up twelve years of accumulated paint in just two hours. The new stand was painted white; the girls had decorated it with multicolored vines and flowers. A large sign proclaimed FRESH-PICKED PRODUCE. It took all of us to carry the finished product down to the mailbox.

On Monday, Sarah's jelly jars of fresh flowers nodded gaily in the morning breeze. Eleanor had piled scrubbed mounds of new potatoes on paper plates. Customers stopped by regularly. But the fun of making change in the noonday sun began to pale. Although the children enjoyed dropping the little piles of change into their piggy banks, they grew weary of turning down invitations to go swimming or bike riding. "Minding the store" was quickly losing its appeal.

"How about using the honor system?" Bob asked one evening.

Three puzzled faces turned to him.

"You see that often at country stands," he explained. "Just list the prices and put out a jar for people to put their money in."

The children looked doubtful but decided to give it a try. Eleanor carefully made a price list. Drew cut a slit in the top of an old jar and Sarah lettered a sign: HONOR JAR. MAKE YOUR OWN CHANGE.

The next day they set up their stand, then returned to the cool of the house and waited. Drew couldn't resist checking the stand at lunchtime. He returned to the house, his face jubilant.

"Half the vegetables are gone and the jar's almost full of money."

By evening only three tomatoes were left. Ever the realist, Drew had made a list of what they put out and what the profit should be. Allowing for the unsold tomatoes, it came out perfectly. Actually, ten cents over.

Excited by the idea of a produce stand that tended itself, the children faithfully harvested the garden each morning and filled the wooden shelves with our bumper crops.

But a week later, as Drew was tallying up the change in the jar, he paused. "I don't think there's enough money here." He looked at me in dismay.

Eleanor and Sarah quickly helped count the pile of change again. Drew checked his list and totaled up what should have been in the jar once more.

"We're $2.40 short," he groaned.

Silence filled the kitchen. My heart ached as I looked at the three sad little faces.

"Maybe some poor people needed food and just didn't have any money," Eleanor said.

"We'll keep the jar out," Drew said firmly. "Maybe I made a mistake."

For three days, the vegetables sold and the money in the jar came out even. But the next evening, Drew and the girls came into the kitchen looking downcast.

"We added it all up, Mom, and someone is taking vegetables again."

I sat down at the table with the children.

"Eleanor was right. Someone probably needed food and just didn't have the money. At least not now."

"It's not like we don't have more than we need for ourselves anyway," Sarah added.

I smiled at her and took a blank card from my recipe box. I made a small sign.

"Would you like to put this by the Honor Jar tomorrow?" I said, handing it to Eleanor.

She read, "If you need vegetables but cannot pay, please help yourself. Or pay later. And may things get better for you soon."

"Would you like to add your signatures at the bottom?" I asked.

The children looked at each other. One by one they signed their names.

In the weeks following, sometimes the Honor Jar was a bit short. But sometimes the change in the jar equaled more than the value of the day's vegetables. At the end of the summer, according to Drew's careful calculations, it had all evened out.

A HARVEST OF T-SHIRTS

A wonderful project for summer family fun is to create T-shirts that celebrate the harvest season. Just dip cut vegetables and fruits into washable fabric paint and press them on T-shirts. Broccoli and cauliflower florets, mushroom halves, citrus wedges, halved apples and pears, and slices of starfruit (carambola), to name just a few, all make great designs. Be creative.

DIRECTIONS:

1. Pour a bit of fabric paint onto a small plate (use separate plates for additional colors).

2. Blot the produce on paper towels to dry its natural juices, then dip lightly into the paint.

3. Using various fruits and vegetables, color combinations, and patterns, experiment on plain paper first. Don't press too hard or the juice of the fruits and vegetables will run.

4. Once you've decided on your color and design, slide some cardboard inside a prewashed cotton T-shirt (so your prints don't bleed through to the back). Pull the sleeves and sides of the shirt firmly around the cardboard and tape them securely with masking tape.

5. Now press the dipped fruits and vegetables slices firmly on the front of the shirt.

6. Let dry. Check both the paint and T-shirt manufacturer's instructions for drying time and care of the shirt.

Memories in a Handbag

While waiting in line at the grocer's recently, I discovered a 1991 receipt from Scoma's Seafood stuffed into my purse. I remembered that I'd gone to San Francisco that October with my husband and had called an old friend to join me for lunch at San Francisco's famous dockside restaurant.

Louisa and I spent hours catching up on each other and swapping stories of our years together in married-student housing. Twenty-one years earlier, I'd taken care of her baby so she and Dave could go to the movies. After rocking Lyn for more than an hour, she and I had fallen asleep together on her parents' bed. Louisa had photographed the two of us as we slumbered and had brought the snapshot to our lunch.

As I stood in the checkout line, holding the crumpled receipt, I was swept back to those simple times when a child's problems could be easily rocked away.

I shouldn't have been surprised to discover that my purse was a miniature time capsule. In my work, I spend hours in libraries and museums and have great respect for archives of all sorts. In the quest for historical documentation, I've pored over such diverse archival material as account books from out-of-business import houses and records for towns that are no longer on the map. One can certainly find history in unusual places. Pocketbooks should be no exception.

That evening, I looked to see what history my other handbags might reveal. Getting them down from the top shelf of my closet, I laid them on the dining room table: a little beaded evening clutch purse, my black over-the-shoulder bag, a summer straw, an old leather satchel.

From the largest of the lot, I shook out an earring that I had given up for lost and an appointment card from the vet for our cat, Feather, who died several years ago.

Feather was our first pet, white and soft as eiderdown. Every winter, she had just two kittens; one of them was always white. We never had trouble finding homes for just two kittens. Then, one year, she had five. We decided to call a halt to our home biology lessons and called the vet.

The summer straw yielded ticket stubs from the merry-go-round at the 1984 County Fair, the last year my daughter would go with me. Thereafter followed a brief period when she was embarrassed to be seen with me at all. She went on the rides with a flock of little girls, their giggles floating out across the twinkling fairgrounds as they teetered on the highest point of the roller coaster. Now, it is young men who take her to the top of the Ferris wheel.

In one of the inside pockets of the satchel, I found a receipt for a day's parking at Atlantic City. We had stopped there on our way to New England and spent a lazy day at the beach watching our children create elaborate sand castles. Later we went to a casino and won thirty dollars—to us, a veritable fortune. We celebrated by buying ice cream cones, which we licked as we strolled along the boardwalk.

The beaded evening bag still contained ticket stubs from Neil Simon's first Broadway play. It's permanently stocked with the basic necessities for an evening on the town: lipstick, a small comb, change for phone calls, and Kleenex (last used, appropriately, at *Les Miserables*).

It took me an hour to empty all the pocketbooks. Like individual archeological digs, they represented years of living and traveling, exciting moments and commonplace comforts. Their contents made a small mound in the middle of the table.

I discarded all the old shopping lists, expired coupons, and broken tea bags. But as I looked at the Paris Metro ticket, the badge from a conference declaring me "President," the directions to a shower for our son's fiancée, I couldn't bear to throw them out. Instead, I shoved them all into a large manila envelope and stuffed it in my bottom desk drawer. As I closed it, a piece of paper became stuck in the glide. Pulling it out I realized that it was an old Christmas card, dated 1974. In the family photograph, our long-married son is missing his two front teeth and his sister, now a sophisticated New Yorker, is wearing her favorite outfit—a frilly dress and cowboy boots. The baby, who is now at a law office in Manhattan, waves from her perch in a backpack.

Tomorrow, I'm starting an archeological dig in my desk.

A Light in the Window

Moving day was drawing to a close. The van rumbled down the lane, leaving us with three hungry children, a frightened cat, and a mountain of boxes to unpack. Our new home seemed vacant and lonely; the nearest neighbor was about a mile down the road. I could see a faint light glimmering through the woods.

Presently, I heard the crunch of tires on gravel; a small pickup truck pulled in beside the barn. When I opened the door, I was greeted by a warm smile. Our new neighbor, Marian, had brought us dinner, friendship, and advice.

My little red address book, full of all the names and numbers a family needs to function, was of no use in this new place. I peppered Marian with questions. Who was a good vet? Where could I find aged manure for the garden? Was there a good plumber in town?

I learned with dismay that the nearest dentist was thirty miles away, but Marian assured me that the drive was beautiful.

She was right. As we drove down the valley, the hills were ablaze with autumn colors. Sugar maples bordered the old stone walls, and yellow willows hung over the stream that meandered alongside the road. In the golden meadows, cows contentedly grazed. We all decided that our favorites were the belted Galloways, whose wide band of white in the middle of their black bodies made us think of Oreo cookies.

By the time we left Dr. Thomasson's office, dusk was beginning to settle. As we passed the edge of town, Drew asked, "Why does each house have a Christmas candle in the window when it isn't even Halloween?"

I remembered that the Snydersville Apple Festival was slated for the coming weekend; we planned to help with the cider pressing. Perhaps this was some sort of tradition, part of the festivities.

That evening, when I called the cat in, she did not come. Kate had been confused ever since the move, meowing forlornly as she wandered through the unfamiliar house. The following morning, she was still missing.

Then winter closed in. The children worried about Kate, and I tried to reassure them that she had probably found a nice warm barn to stay in for the winter. She was hibernating, I said, like a bear.

Mud season delayed the plowing. Spring chores piled up. Finally, one warm March afternoon as the first daffodils were blooming, the children and I headed back to Snydersville to buy new shoes. Sarah couldn't decide between the red sneakers or the white, and Eleanor took a long time finding just the right pair of party shoes. It was growing late by the time we left for home. Dusk was beginning to fall.

"Look," said Eleanor as we neared the outskirts of the village, "those houses still have lights in the window."

We saw that four or five houses on the left side of the road and three on the right all had a single candle lit.

I asked Marian if she knew why, and she answered, "It's the way it's always been." Then she laughed. "That's a common answer to a lot of questions around here."

The following month, while the children were being seen by Dr. Thomasson, I asked his nurse if she knew the answer to the mystery.

She just shrugged and replied, "That's the way it has always been."

I hid a small smile.

"Excuse me," a voice behind me said.

I turned around. An elderly lady in a green print dress motioned to me from a sofa in the waiting room.

"Come sit by me," she said, patting the seat beside her. "I'd be happy to tell you about those candles. I'm Grace Harding, and I live in the last house on the left. You know, the little red one?"

"Yes," I said. "I admired your beautiful bank of forsythia on the way into town."

"Forty years ago, when I married Henry and came to Snydersville, the first people to welcome us were the Johnsons, Clem and Anna. They had the farmhouse set back from the road."

I had seen the neat, white frame building set among its barns and outbuildings like a mother hen surrounded by her chicks.

"They had two sons, Arthur, the elder, a strong helpful boy who took after his father, and James, a quiet sort. He liked to read books.

He's a professor over at the state college now." She smiled at Sarah who was sitting beside me, listening intently.

"When we began to have children, their daughter, Mary, used to mind them if we went to the cinema.

"Well, the war came along, and Arthur signed up. It nearly tore Anna apart, him being her firstborn and all. But he wouldn't be dissuaded. James stayed home and helped his father run the farm." She sighed. "A lot of the village boys went off to war."

Drawing herself back to her story, she continued, "Arthur wrote home regularly, and Anna used to read his letters to all the neighbors. She was very proud of him but worried, nonetheless. Mothers do that."

I nodded in agreement.

"About a year after he'd left, the letters stopped coming. Anna was just frantic. Then a man from the war office came by to tell them that Arthur was missing in action. They didn't know if he had been taken prisoner or . . ." Her voice trailed off as she looked at Sarah, who was holding my hand tightly.

"That evening, Anna left the porch light on all night. Told Clem that she wouldn't turn it off until Arthur came home. A few days later I noticed that Ella Winter, down the road, had left her light on, too. So had the Moores. At twilight, I turned on a small lamp in my front window. It was the least I could do."

"How long did she have to leave the porch light on?" I asked, half dreading her response.

"Until she died," she answered in a soft voice. "After Arthur had been reported missing, I went to pay a visit. When I turned to go, I noticed a big piece of tape over the switch to the porch light. Anna looked at it. 'No one touches that switch,' she said to me. 'Clem tried to turn it off one morning but I stopped him. Told him I didn't care about the electricity.'"

Mrs. Harding looked at Sarah and continued. "A few years later, those little electric Christmas candles came out, and the neighbors and I began burning them in our windows. We left them on for Arthur." She paused and then added, "And for all the others."

"The farmhouse still has its porch light on, doesn't it?" asked Sarah.

"Yes, dear," Mrs. Harding replied. "James lives in his parents' house now. The tape is still over the switch."

"Do you think Arthur might come back someday?" asked Sarah, her face full of worry.

"He might," Mrs. Harding said quietly.

"But he'd be very old, wouldn't he?" said Sarah.

"Yes, dear. He would be."

That evening after supper, I heard noises in the attic and felt the cool draft that always means someone has left the door at the top of the stairs open.

"Who's up there?" I called.

"Just me," Sarah's muffled voice responded.

She came down the stairs with one of our window candles in her hand.

"I know it isn't Christmas yet, but I really want to put this in my window," she said, with a look that was at once hopeful and resolute.

"For Arthur?" I asked.

"Well, sort of," Sarah said. "But mostly for Kate. Maybe she's lost and just needs a light to guide her home."

I could not say no.

After I tucked her in, I stood in the doorway and looked at the candle.

Two weeks later, Kate returned followed by three kittens. Where she'd been, we'll never know. We were just glad to have her back.

"Can we leave the light on?" asked Sarah when we settled Kate into her basket. I nodded. For Arthur. And for all the others.

A Candle in the Darkness

If you and your children would like to make your own Christmas light, just gather some sturdy cardboard, some heavy aluminum foil (or aluminum pie tins), a long tie twist, and a single plastic candle with an electric cord and a bulb.

Cut out a star about five inches tall from the cardboard (or pie tin) and punch two holes in one of the points. Cover the star with tinfoil on all sides, pierce the foil where you've made the holes in the cardboard, and thread the tie twist through. Fasten the star tightly to the plastic base of the candle, just below and in front of the bulb. Plug in the candle and be sure the cord is safely tucked out of reach.

When the light is placed on your windowsill, passersby will see a soft glow surrounding a dark star. To appreciate these halos from inside, you can fasten another star on the inside of the candle as well. For a more openwork look, pierce holes in the star randomly or in a pattern with an ice pick or nail or paper punch. You can attach the star permanently to the candle with a hot-glue gun, but you might prefer changing the shapes with the seasons: a snowflake, a heart, a flower, a shell, or an oak leaf. That way you can keep your light in the window burning all year long, too.

Nesting

L ast month, I hung an old rag rug over my porch railing to dry. A few minutes later, a little sparrow began pulling at the fringe, finding the soft cotton threads perfect for her nesting needs.

Birds are opportunists. In seeking to make strong, yet comfortable nests for their young, they do not hesitate to use materials from both nature, like grasses, moss, and twigs, and man, such as yarn, rags, and paper napkins. The straw I used to mulch my asparagus quickly became a nest-maker's delight. And nesting birds often shred the string I use to tie up the hollyhocks.

Early this morning, on my way to the garden, I noticed that the first bluebird fledglings had flown from their nesting box. I raised the top of their little house on the fence post and carefully lifted out the nest. Bluebirds claim a nesting box for their own and return to it year after year. We've discovered that if we clean out the nest as soon as the fledglings have flown, their parents may build another and raise as many as three families each summer.

Whenever I clean out the dryer's lint trap or brush our cat I take the resulting fluff to the edge of the woods and scatter it on a bush in the hopes that some bird will find it useful. It is my thank-you to them for filling these same woods with song.

As I clean out the various nesting boxes we have around the place, I sometimes do see evidence that the things I've set out for the birds have been incorporated into nests. But just as often I find surprises.

Last year, a little jenny wren found her way into my garden shed and built a nest in my raspberry bucket. When July came and it was time to gather berries, I got the bucket down and pulled out a nest partially made of green ribbons, the kind that curl when pulled against a scissor's edge.

The titmice in the birdhouse by the barn had incorporated some thin orange streamers into their nest. The long paper strands looked as though they had come from a cheerleader's pom-pom. And some ruby finches made a nest in a basket of impatiens on the porch. Their nestlings had a glorious canopy of red flowers for a roof. I took great care not to disturb them as I carefully watered the flowers. *Perhaps,* I thought, *they'll just believe that I am a small rainstorm.* When the last baby had fledged, I removed the nest and found that the finches had woven into it faded cellophane "grass" from a child's Easter basket.

My husband is amused that I save dryer fluff and bits of string and yarn for the birds. I shall have to show him this bluebird nest.

Cradling it gently in my hand, I head back to the house to start breakfast. As I pass through the front hall, I catch my reflection in the oval mirror that hangs there. I found the mirror in New York City when my son was a baby. It was propped up against the steps of an old brownstone along with a tattered rug and a broken umbrella stand. I stopped short. I remembered that it was "Big Junk Night" in Manhattan but I couldn't believe that someone was throwing away this wonderful old mirror. The lady who lived in the house came out to add some more things to the pile.

"Do you like that mirror, dear?" she asked. I nodded.

"Then it's yours," she said as she helped me place it crosswise on the pram. Holding it steady, I carefully pushed Drew and the mirror the three blocks home.

Thus began my career as a lover of "found objects" (or "ragpicker," as my husband affectionately calls me). When our drugstore closed after ninety-four years of business, I found the owner putting out a box of old apothecary jars. Most were cracked or missing their glass stoppers, but he helped me find several that still had their original gilt labels. I carried home two and, with directions from the clerk at the hardware store, turned them into small table lamps. An old treadle sewing machine, minus its battered cabinet, became a base for a table. A faded blanket was washed and given a new cover, hand-tied in place with yarn. Fifteen years later, it still keeps us warm.

When we bought our first house, I haunted thrift shops and combed tag sales. I made pillows out of the usable bits of tattered quilts, and sewed curtains from old sheets whose once brilliant colors had faded to pleasing, muted shades.

"You certainly are a nester," my mother remarked one day as she helped me slipcover an armchair a neighbor had put out for the trash man (and which I had coerced my husband into rescuing under cover of darkness).

Her words come back to me as I gaze at my reflection in the hall mirror. "One man's trash is another man's treasure," I had replied to her then. Now, looking down at the nest in my hand, I wonder: Perhaps that should be "One creature's trash is another creature's treasure."

The buzz of the dryer signals the end of a load. I take out the warm clothes and place them in a basket. Then, I pull out the lint trap and brush off a handful of fluff. After dinner I'll take it into the woods. It's still early in the season. Perhaps the bluebirds will find it.

LENDING A HAND

Birds, of course, have been building nests without our help for eons. But children love to feel that they have a part in helping them. A good rainy-day activity for spring months is to create a "nesting supply box." With your children, hunt through your house for bits of string and yarn, excelsior and shredded paper. Soft rags can be torn into thin strips and, of course, the dryer can be mined for lint. Put small amounts of these materials in an out-of-the way spot in your yard, high up in a bush or tree, or perhaps on the railing of an apartment balcony, and watch it disappear. It is fun to see what the birds like best. Replenish the materials as they disappear or become overly dampened by rains. By August, you can take in what has not been used, for, as the first cool mornings appear, the birds' nest building draws to a close. And just like people, many of them head south for warmer climes!

The Measuring Stick

I t was time to repaint the kitchen. One evening, while sitting at the dinner table, my husband and I were discussing the pros and cons of various colors for walls and trim. The children, deep in discussions about a western camping trip, suddenly stopped their lively conversation. Horror filled their faces. In one voice they all cried, "Not the measuring stick!"

"No," I reassured them calmly in my best mother-has-everything-under-control voice. "Not the measuring stick."

The measuring stick isn't really a stick but the kitchen side of the door that stands between the kitchen and the dining room. Through the years, along the door's edge, we've made little marks celebrating each child's growth. Every birthday is duly noted and the child's height for that year carefully written beside it. Over the decades, so many various-colored pens, pencils, and markers were used to make the notes that the door came to vaguely resemble an abstract expressionist painting.

The names and dates are in many different handwritings. I can tell by the script just who measured whom. An eight-year-old measured her three-year-old sister, a grandchild measured her grandmother, my husband measured me (although, at forty, I demurred that I didn't need to be measured anymore!).

It isn't just family whose heights are noted on the door. At parties, when the door swings back and forth frequently, friends often stop to read the various names and dates. When we catch them at it, we add their names and dates to the chronicle. For a while, the highest mark on the door belonged to neighbor Bill Marmon. But then Jack Benjamin came to dinner and topped him by an inch.

Many of those listed on the door are still growing; some have stopped. And some whose names are written there remain with us only in memory. When my daughter's friend Kristen brought her grandmother over for tea, the elder woman's height was duly noted. In fancy, teenage script, I read "Gummy, 1992." I recall how she admired our spring flowers, her exclamations of delight made all the more memorable by the softness of her Irish brogue. She died the following winter. When my mother came to see our oldest daughter graduate from college, we measured her, too. It was her last visit to our home.

It was at my husband's parents' house that I first saw such a measuring stick. I remember how odd I thought it looked to have the molding around the kitchen door painted white except for one piece that was still the original bare pine covered with pencil marks.

When my husband was twelve, his family had begun to build a new house. His excitement at finally getting a room of his own and a driveway with room for a basketball hoop could hardly be contained. Each day, after school, he would ride his bike over to the house to see what was new. One afternoon, one of the builders stood him against the new molding, placed a carpenter's level on his head, drew a bold line and wrote "Bobby Bedford, 1955."

That inscription is still there. After forty years, the doorjamb has still not been painted; no one has had the heart. Young Bobby's measurement has been joined by dozens of others, including one for me, as a sweetheart and another as his (slightly taller) wife. Our children have been proudly recorded on the woodwork by their grandparents, and even the family cat has a mark.

Sometimes, when friends see our gaily "decorated" door, their eyes widen in surprise (or is it horror?).

"You let the children write all over that door?" they ask.

I simply smile and nod. Then I pick up a pencil and ask them if they would like to be immortalized, too. They usually grin sheepishly, slip off their shoes, and back right into place.

As our children were growing up, they frequently felt that they had to "measure up." A difficult thing. Their teachers often expected them by to be just like (or not like) an older sibling. And they wondered whether or not they would ever achieve a fraction of the things their heroes or heroines had achieved. Sometimes, they were compared to their parents or grandparents. It is hard, when you are only ten or thirteen, to measure up to someone who is forty or sixty-two. But on the measuring stick it is easy to see just how you measure up to yourself.

Each year on the morning of our children's birthdays, they get to see just how far they've come in the last year. Sometimes it is just half an inch; between our son's fourteenth and fifteenth birthday, it was three!

But, by the time the older ones stopped growing, they had usually stopped trying to measure up; they were content with who they were. Their personal measuring sticks had become spiritual and intellectual. Inner growth replaced outer.

We haven't quite decided on the color scheme for the kitchen—yet. But one thing is certain. If we should paint the trim curry gold, Chowning Tavern red, or federal blue, the back of the kitchen door will always remain white. White, with lots of names and dates in assorted colors.

Big Oaks from Little Acorns Grow

It's fun to keep track of everyone's growth—children's as well as adults'. A family measuring stick can take many forms. It can be a simple series of marks on a door-jamb or door, or a fanciful mural of a tree on a child's wall with a new branch for each year of growth. Some parents have sewn a long, narrow piece of cloth and tacked it to a wall or door. On this, in permanent marker, each child's height is listed. This sort of growth chart can be as plain or fancy as you wish, but the advantage of a portable measuring stick like this is that you can take it with you if you move from your present home to a new one.

Eye of the Beholder

C ousin Becca is visiting for Garden Week, that wonderful time in the spring when Virginia's historic gardens are open to the public. She's made the journey for many reasons: to have a preview of a spring that is, for her, still many weeks away, to thaw out a bit from a particularly fierce New England winter, and to spend a few quiet days simply sitting on our back porch.

Cousin Becca is actually my grandmother's cousin. We are, she once told me, first cousins, twice removed. She taught me the intricacies of familial relationships so that I can now immediately identify a particular cousin by the proper title, a handy skill in a family with hundreds of cousins of all descriptions scattered from Maine to California. I just met a third cousin from Mobile, Alabama and am currently corresponding with a fourth cousin, once removed. But we are all descended from the same hardy New Englanders.

A few years back, when I was making many trips to Massachusetts to research a book, Cousin Becca's guest room became my northern home. After a wonderful dinner of clams or cod, we would sit on her tiny balcony overlooking Marblehead Harbor and talk of our mutual ancestors and family. I brought her honey from my bees.

As we sat there, sipping our honey-sweetened Lapsang souchong and watching the little boats bobbing at anchor, she would tell me stories of the generations that went before us and of the history of the New England town from which they had come. Not a visit would go by that I did not discover three or four new things about our family. Not a visit would pass that I did not press her to visit us in Virginia.

At last she has let me return her hospitality, to serve her meals that I hope are as delicious as those she served me. The view from my porch is not of gently lapping waves but of dusky blue mountains and deep purple valleys. She enjoys it just the same.

Today we visited two grand estates with acres of tulips and forget-me-nots, azaleas, and creeping phlox. Gravel paths wound past elegant ponds with gently splashing fountains. We caught glimpses of two or three full-time gardeners discreetly clipping and pruning.

"Show me your gardens, dear," said Cousin Becca, when we had returned home.

"Oh, they're really not much," I sighed. After the manicured beds and formal arrangements of our day's outing, my humble gardens looked amateurish by comparison.

"But they're lovely," she protested. "I can see that from here."

Looking across the drive, she said, "See how effective the iris and daisies are against that drift of pink and rose azaleas." She swept her hand to include some hemlocks I'd planted seven years ago. "And I love the way the texture of those evergreens is such a wonderful counterpoint to the shape of the viburnum."

And turning, I could see that she was right. From a distance, the border of azaleas made a perfect backdrop for the perennials. The white flowers of the viburnum were cool against the dark green hemlocks. I realized that, from the front steps, Cousin Becca could see neither the weeds nor the patches of bare earth.

As we walked to the door, I saw my gardens with a fresh eye. "Just don't look too closely," I laughed.

She smiled and replied, "Beauty does not often bear close scrutiny."

While Cousin Becca went in to start tea, I gathered an armful of flowers to make a bouquet for the dinner table. When I came into the kitchen, she and my daughter, Sarah, were looking over Sarah's yearbook.

Cousin Becca looked up. "Bleeding hearts!" she exclaimed on seeing my collection of blooms. "Such a lovely, old-fashioned flower."

Putting the bouquet into a vase of water, I pulled out a stem of bleeding hearts and gave it to her.

"You know how to find the bunnies in these, don't you, dear?" she asked Sarah.

My daughter and I exchanged puzzled looks. We had made hollyhock dancers and daisy chains. We'd tested each other with buttercups to see if we liked butter and made elderflower fritters. But bunnies in the bleeding hearts? Sarah shook her head.

Cousin Becca gently pulled apart a blossom. "Here are the two bunnies," she said laying two pale pink shapes on the kitchen table, "and here are two ballet slippers and a perfume flask."

The stamen and pistil of the flower did, indeed, look just like dancing shoes and a tall, thin bottle. Enchanted, Sarah plucked off another blossom and separated it into its various parts.

I set the vase on the counter and joined them. While the fragrance of the flowers filled the air, the kitchen table quickly became covered with tiny pink bits. But the graceful stem of bleeding hearts was gone, its natural elegance destroyed. Although the effect of the whole was lovely, its dissected parts were merely oddities that provoked in me a certain sadness.

The delightful fragrance of the spring bouquet, coupled with an odd sense of disappointment, reminded me of a birthday party I had gone to in third grade. It was May, and all the gardens in town were bursting with flowers. I walked to the party very slowly so that I could enjoy the sweet smell of each yard. When I reached Priscilla's house, her mother opened the door and showed me into the living room, where all the other girls had gathered around the coffee table. On it was a pile of presents and a beautiful bouquet. I couldn't resist; I plunged my face in and breathed deeply of the fragrance.

But there was none. The blossoms were made of silk. I pulled back in astonishment and surprise. The other girls howled with laughter. My shock and surprise were instantly replaced by embarrassment. When I grew up, I silently vowed, I would never have silk flowers in my house.

When I told this story to Becca and Sarah, they nodded and allowed as to how it was easy to be confused by an imitation, especially a beautiful one.

Cousin Becca recalled, "My niece Hariette—now she would be your second cousin, once removed—told me a story of going to her friend's house for a vacation. The family had gathered on the screen porch for tea. Hariette went over to a large window that looked out on a beautiful view, so that she could open the curtain a bit wider and see more of the lovely scenery. But when she put her hand to the fabric, she bumped into solid wood." Becca laughed at the memory of the tale. "Poor Hariette, it was a trompe l'oeil painting. Her friend's little brother nearly fell off the settee with laughter."

"What did she do?" asked Sarah, all too aware of the agonies of mortification.

Cousin Becca smiled, "Her hostess stifled the little boy's mirth with one swift glance and merely said, 'Everyone mistakes that for a real window, dear. The artist who painted it takes such errors as the highest form of compliment.'"

Cousin Becca and I took our tea out to the porch. Now, as we sit there, the shadows lengthen across the valley. Cousin Becca admires the mountains, their gentle slopes enfolded in a mantle of dusk. But I am distracted. I see the dead tree that I should take down, hear the interruption of a distant highway, object to the radio tower just barely visible on Calf Pasture Mountain.

Most days, I overlook these things; I know they are there, but I have ceased to focus on them. Now that I have a guest, though, I am aware of my view's shortcomings. I begin to apologize for the defects in the landscape, but Cousin Becca puts her fingers to her lips. A wood thrush fills the air with his twilight song. I remain silent, for it is clear she doesn't notice the faults; she takes in only beauty.

I remember Becca's wonderful view of the Marblehead harbor. Perhaps the boats needed painting; maybe the concrete jetty was an unnatural intrusion. I did not notice, for the effect of the whole charmed me.

We are content, sitting here sipping our tea and admiring nature's handiwork. The sun begins to set behind the mountains, the dead pine becomes a graceful, black silhouette against the pink and gold clouds, a striking bonsai, part of the grand design.

Cousin Becca is right. Beauty should not be subjected to close scrutiny.

Fun with Flowers

Ever made a snapdragon snap? Did you know a flower can tell if you like butter? Flowers lend themselves to all sorts of fun.

A hibiscus, minus its petals, makes a great "tickler," says my niece Lily, and it will stay open all day without water, making it a perfect flower to stick behind the ear of a child who wants to be a Hawaiian prince or princess. To make a daisy (or dandelion) chain, pick flowers with long stems. Cut a tiny slit in the stem about a half-inch below the flower and thread the stem of the next flower through this. Repeat the process until you have a long chain. Tie the ends together to create a necklace or a crown.

Hollyhock dancers can be made with two blooms. Put one flower face down on a table and cut a small slit in the stem end. Then, fold the petals of the other bloom carefully downward away from the stamen (that's the dancer's head), and push its stem end into the first flower. Tie a long piece of grass around the middle of these bent-back petals to secure the two flowers together and create a belt for your dancer's dress. You can thread another piece of grass between the petals of the upper flower if you'd like your dancer to have arms.

Golden yellow buttercups will tell you if you like butter. On a sunny day, pick one and hold it beneath your chin. Ask your child to see if a patch of yellow appears under your chin. If it does, you like butter! A snapdragon blossom can become a mighty dragon if you gently squeeze his "cheeks" on either side of his "mouth" (the opening of the bloom). Several children with several blooms can create a wonderful puppet show. Look for the funny faces in violets and pansies. Putting pieces of various flowers together to create funny faces or odd creatures helps kids learn about the scientific names of various flower parts.

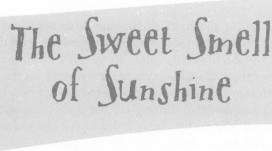

The Sweet Smell of Sunshine

"Good morning," I say as I hear my sister's step on the stair. "Did the smell of the biscuits wake you?"

Ellen smiles. "No, I've been up for a bit. But speaking of aromas, what do you wash your sheets in? They have such a wonderful scent."

"That's the smell of sunshine."

Ellen looks puzzled. "A new detergent?" she asked. "I haven't heard of that one."

"No," I laugh and point to my clothesline, strung between two trees in the backyard. "I hang my laundry out on that line. The combination of the fresh breezes and sun dry them in no time."

I press a linen tea towel to my face and breathe deeply. "And I love the way it smells."

"I'd forgotten clotheslines," Ellen says with a smile. "Remember when we used to help Grandy hang out the clothes?"

Our grandmother hung her laundry out on a line strung between her house and her barn. The line hung in a neat coil on the side of the barn for most of the week but, on Mondays, she would pull it out taut and fasten it to a large metal hook on her house. If we were around on washday, she would dub us "Mistresses of the Pins" and tie her clothespin aprons—yellow calico with red rickrack on the pockets—around our waists.

From a distance, our rhythm must have looked like a lovely pas de deux. Grandy bending gracefully down to the wicker basket, pulling out a piece of laundry, giving it a sharp snap to straighten it out, and placing it over the line. I reaching up to hand her the clothespins.

When I had children of my own, I loved hanging the tiny baby clothes and diapers on the line and gathering them in a few hours later, sweet-smelling and fresh. Something about sunshine seemed to keep the girls' batiste baby dresses sparkling white. And the diapers were so easy to fold, dried smooth as they were by the wind.

Sometimes the clothesline provided live theater for the children.

"Look, Mommy," they would giggle as they gazed out the window. "The clothes are dancing." Sitting on the window seat, we would watch together as my husband's jeans did high kicks and my nighties swayed back and forth, waving their arms in graceful arcs.

The clothes on the line often serve as a sort of barometer, warning me of an impending storm. As a low pressure system moves in, the clothes hang limply from their pins. Then, as the storm approaches, they begin to flap, not with the regular, undulating wave of a steady, drying breeze but with a nervous twitching. When they begin to whip about wildly, I race out to gather them in before the rain hits. Often, I get the laundry into the basket in the nick of time, and big drops pelt me as I streak for the house.

Sometimes, I am too late. Distracted by some other chore or deeply engrossed in writing, I do not realize a storm is upon me until I hear the first clap of thunder.

"The laundry!" I'll gasp as I run to the door, only to be stopped by a curtain of rain. I slump against the window, watching the rain sluice from the sky, drenching the clothes. There they hang, poor things, water pouring into pants pockets, rain running in rivulets down the shirts.

But there's something about clothes that have had a final rinse of rain. When the sun breaks through and they are dry for a second time, they have a special fragrance—sort of spicy and sweet combined.

Occasionally I will forget to bring the laundry in at night. If the moon is full, the clothes look like phantoms blowing and moving eerily in the moonlit air.

"Look," I would say to the children. "There are ghosts in the backyard."

"Ghosts?!!" they would shout and run to the windows.

"Oh, Mom," they would groan in unison when they beheld my so-called spirits. I was only able to pull that off two or three times.

The children used my clothesline, too. When two sheets were pinned up, they made a perfect curtain for the Bedford Family Players.

Although it may not have been a heavy sweep of red velvet, many a young actress or actor has made an entrance from behind that improvised curtain. Several appreciative audiences have gathered on blankets or in lawn chairs to watch a neighborhood production of *Swan Lake* or *Little Red Riding Hood*.

The clothesline became an integral part of the children's outdoor "let's pretend." If I lowered the line a bit, we could drape an old double bed sheet over it, secure the corners with stones, and voilà—a tent! The children would fill it with pillows and dolls, tea sets and dress-ups, and, pretty soon, they were camping in the wilderness on their way west to discover gold in the California mountains, the tent keeping them safe from (teddy) bears.

"Don't you have a dryer?" Ellen asks as we take our breakfast tea outside to enjoy the warm summer sunshine.

"I do," I answer. "But I really prefer my solar-powered one. Hanging the clothes on the line saves electricity, and I don't have to iron as much."

Ellen nods and then adds, "The clothes do smell wonderful."

I smile in agreement and then think of another benefit. "Besides," I laugh, "all that bending down to the basket and reaching up to the line has got to be good for my waist."

DANCE OF THE CLOTHESPINS

One of the wonderful side benefits of having a clothesline is the clothespins—they make wonderful dolls. Get yourself a package of the old-fashioned clothespins (not the spring type) and a package of pipe cleaners. With a magic marker, paint a face on the round top of the clothespin. Now, to make arms, cut a pipe cleaner to about three inches and twist it around the "neck" of the doll. For a boy doll, draw in details of a shirt, belt and blacken the "leg" of the clothespin to make his pants. For a girl doll, cut a circle of fabric and make a small hole in the center. Slip it over the "head" of your doll and hold in place around the neck of the doll with the pipe cleaner arms. If you want to get more elaborate, a bit of glued yarn makes wonderful "hair" and a bit of lace a lovely hat. Let your children use their imaginations and be prepared to behold some elegant creations.

Truck City

My small herb and honey farm had grown to the point where I needed a large vehicle of some sort to move hives and deliver orders. Nothing fancy, mind you, just big. So early one Saturday morning, my husband and I made the round of the used-car lots on the strip north of town known locally as "Hamburger Alley." Our last stop was Truck City.

A salesman in a blue plaid shirt and a red "Truck City" cap found us poking about the used pickups. We'd already worked our way through the selection of vans with plush seats that swiveled 360 degrees, mini blinds at the windows, television sets front and back, with names like The Cruiser, Fun Wagon, and Don's Delight emblazoned on the rear cargo door. We'd gone past what I can only describe as monster trucks, with little pickup bodies towering atop huge, forty-inch tires. They had roll bars and racks of spotlights encased in yellow covers with smiley faces on them.

"Howdy folks," a salesman grinned. "Findin' what ya want?"

When we admitted that the price tags on even the humblest of the basic-model trucks put them beyond our reach, the friendly fellow, who'd introduced himself as Billy, led us to what appeared to be a sort of "scratch-and-dent" corner in the back of the lot.

"Now, this here's the baby for ya," he said, as he patted the bright orange hood of a '76 Chevy half-ton. Watching my husband check it over, open the hood, and kick the tires, I was reminded of how my mother had carefully examined the teeth and legs of a pony she had once bought my little sister. I was pleased that the upholstery was intact and there was room for three kids in the cab. The dents were minor, and the missing bumper didn't bother me much. This was going to be a working truck, after all. The mileage was low, too. Only later was I to discover why. It barely got nine miles to the gallon.

We haggled a bit on the price, and, when Billy said he would throw two Truck City caps in with the purchase, we told him he had a deal. As my husband put on his new cap and got into our old sedan for the ride home, I told him he looked just like Richard Petty. He grinned sheepishly, gunned the engine, and took off.

Hanging my own cap on the gun rack that stretched across the back window, I climbed up into the cab of my new truck and pulled out into traffic. Immediately it became evident that, in my Chevy half-ton, I commanded respect. Other drivers were only too happy to allow me onto the highway. Traffic circles were a breeze. Maybe all those dents made me look like I had nothing to lose. Or, maybe it was because my truck was so big. I felt like I was about twelve feet off the ground. After years of driving Volkswagens and Hondas, being able to look down on all the other cars was a new sensation. A feeling of power gripped me. I thought about getting a CB.

At home, my new truck received rather mixed reviews. "Far out, man," was our seventeen-year-old son's reaction—his highest accolade. I could see Drew had great plans.

"Mother, how could you?" Wailed our thirteen-year old daughter. Eleanor swore she was going to die of embarrassment. Nobody's mother drove a truck, and she vowed never to ride in it. Of course, as time went by, there were times when she had to ride with me in the pickup, but on those occasions, she would slide down in the seat every time she spotted a familiar car approaching. Our youngest thought the truck was definitely "neat."

When it was parked beneath the tree that held Sarah's swing and her tree house, its bed often became an extension of her outdoor world. Usually, it was turned into a fort or a desert outpost. Occasionally, it appeared to be a mobile classroom. Several times, before I could use it, I would have to remove from the back several pallets and remnants of sheet "bandages," testimony to its having been used as a field hospital.

To make the truck's accoutrements better suited to my personal style, I covered the N.R.A. decal with a Nature Conservancy oak leaf. Although we didn't really need the gun rack, which was welded on, we soon discovered it was perfect for tennis racquets and fly rods.

The truck became an immediate hit with friends and neighbors. It was borrowed frequently. When I wasn't moving hives or delivering honey, we loaned it to haul mulch and manure, make runs to the dump, deliver kids to college, or carry canoes to the river. Our minister turned it into a moving van, and it's also taken apples to the cider press and lambs to the country fair. It's delivered firewood to a couple with a new woodstove. A friend who is an inventor borrowed it to move a quarter-ton "secret" in the dark of night. It's carried carolers through the snow and a Brownie troop on a hayride.

Before long, I began to wonder how we'd ever gotten along without a truck. It was incredibly practical and I had to admit I enjoyed the sheer size of a pickup. I figured if I ever had a showdown with anything smaller than a Mack truck, I'd stand a pretty good chance of winning.

I knew the friends who asked me when I was going to graduate to the big rigs, secretly envied me my ultimate station wagon. But, perhaps the most enjoyable side benefit of becoming the driver of a pickup truck has been the sense of acceptance into a whole new club. There's a sort of camaraderie among those who drive pickup trucks. As I drive down the back roads near our home, people who never even glanced up when I went by in my little Honda wave to me. And, when I pull into a rural gas station at the same time as, say, a Buick or a Mercedes, I always get filled up first.

Chopsticks and Pumpkin Pie

O ne of the best things about living near a college town is the chance to share in the diverse cultural backgrounds of the students. Grocery stores are full of exotic foods to sample and festivals of international music delight students and townspeople—young and old alike. Our children were fascinated by West African drumming, laughed at Japanese shadow puppets, and clapped in time to Greek folk dancing. Eleanor and Sarah, our aspiring ballerinas, were enchanted by graceful Indonesian dances. Our son Drew admired the demonstrations of tae kwon do. Our church, which was within walking distance of the campus, always had international students in attendance.

Perhaps it was all this exposure to the world's diverse cultures that inspired our daughter Eleanor to spend her senior year in high school in a small town in France. She was excited at the prospect, but when the reality of being a stranger in a strange land descended on her, we received many a tearful telephone call. Her homesickness proved short lived, however, for her sponsor, Anne de Surmont, found a wonderful French family that welcomed Eleanor into their hearts and home. Our sense of relief and gratitude was overwhelming when Eleanor called to tell us she was actually dreaming in French, loved the little village of Sorbiers, and might never come home.

One Sunday morning my husband and I were reading the papers when a small announcement caught my eye. Maybe it was my wish to repay a global debt of gratitude that caused me to quickly scan the article. "Listen to this," I said excitedly, reading Bob the headline. "Host families needed for incoming international students."

He smiled and gave me a thumbs-up.

The next morning, the director of International House ushered me into his office and told me about the host-family program. As we talked, I gazed about his brightly decorated office. African wood carvings sat on a shelf, flanking a set of nesting Russian dolls; flags from dozens of countries dangled from the curtain rod; batik hangings in brilliant reds and purples festooned his walls. On his desk, a small jade Buddha sat on top of a basket that looked as though it might have come from Thailand.

"Basically, we hope that host families will help their students learn their way around town," he explained. "Get them settled into their apartments, show them the ropes."

"Can we have them to our house for dinner?" I asked. "Take them bike riding? To concerts and movies?"

"Absolutely," the director enthused. "That's just what we hope you will do. Treat them like your own children." He showed me pictures of some of the international students he had hosted over the years, playing volleyball with his kids, canoeing down the river, hiking the Blue Ridge Mountains. "They are all eager to learn about America. Most of what they know comes from movies and television."

I rolled my eyes and groaned.

"Right," he said, shaking his head. "We hope that you will be able to show them what our country is *really* like."

That evening we had a lively discussion about including a foreign student in our family. The children vividly remembered how they felt when they were the new kid in school or just starting camp or entering a new ballet class or Girl Scout troop. They were eager to help someone from another country adjust to all the overwhelming newness.

After we cleared the dishes, I spread the student profiles the director had given me out on the dining-room table. There was a young man from Pakistan who would be studying engineering, a freshman from Brazil, two sisters from Ireland who were entering the nursing school. We all decided on Yu-Li, a young woman from Taiwan who planned to study economics.

Over the summer we exchanged letters. Yu-Li told us she liked to hike and swim, had two little sisters (our daughters were thrilled), and loved to cook (we all hoped for some true Szechwan recipes). We helped her get settled into her apartment. Her roommates were a young woman from Indonesia who was studying architecture and another from India who wanted to be a physicist. Yu-Li had spent a summer in Great Britain as a child, and her English had a delightful clip to it.

Over the next few months, we introduced Yu-Li to Mozart and bowling, tubing down the James River, and American birthday parties. In exchange, she showed us how to make dim sum and authentic Chinese stir-fry. She attended a potluck supper at our church, and we attended a concert of Chinese music given by the Asian Student Society. When her mother came for a visit, they prepared us a delicious, eight-course Mandarin dinner. Through Yu-Li, her mother thanked us for taking care of her daughter. I shook my head and asked Yu-Li to please tell her mother that we thanked her for sharing her daughter with us. The tears that sprang up in her eyes spoke more than any words, for I recognized a fellow parent who found it hard to send a child far across the sea.

When we invited Yu-Li to share Thanksgiving with us, she asked if she might bring her brother, who was visiting. "Of course," we said. "The more the merrier."

Chou-en spoke little English but was an engaging conversationalist, nonetheless, and was fascinated with the history of Thanksgiving. I offered him chopsticks, which he gratefully accepted. We were all spellbound by his effortless grace in chasing a cranberry around his plate and neatly adding it to a piece of turkey. Somehow he managed to scoop up every morsel of pumpkin pie—whipped cream included.

When Yu-Li returned home to Taiwan, we became a host family to Gladys from Mexico. She, too, was studying economics. Gladys brought us bags woven by the people of her village and taught us just what to order at the local Mexican restaurant. We are sure that, one day, we will hear that she has become the first woman secretary of the treasury of Mexico.

Shortly after Gladys graduated, our children's high school asked us if we would take in two sisters from Korea while their mother found work and a home here. Drew had gone off to college, so they slept in his old bunk beds and delighted us with their flawless piano playing and knowledge of operatic arias. Their first semester here, speaking little English, they both made straight A's. Their constant studying awed our children, but they both learned to fit in some time for just plain fun. We introduced them to pizza; they stocked our refrigerator with triple-wrapped kim chi. We coaxed them away from their desks to swim and sail at a nearby lake, and they kept our tables full of graceful flower arrangements.

When we hosted Ann, a student from Switzerland, we had frequent fondue parties in her honor. To these, we often invited another freshman, the son of friends from Utah. Joshua's home was in the mountains, too, so we figured he was almost as good as Swiss. He may not have been international, but we adopted him, anyway.

Last summer we received another Asian daughter. Yufei, an aspiring electrical engineer, is from the Republic of China. On her first day in America, we invited her to our house for a typical American barbecue: grilled chicken, tossed salad, and corn on the cob. She looked puzzled. Picking up her knife and fork, she said shyly, "I have never used these before." I offered to fetch her some chopsticks. "No," she replied with a determined smile. "I am in America now. I must learn how to use these."

The chicken nearly slid off her plate before she managed to carve a small bite. She held it triumphantly in the air on the tines of her fork and said, "Success!" We all clapped.

Through the years, our international students have created in us an awareness of the smallness of our planet, the similarities among all people. We now read the newspaper with a heightened awareness of the affairs of countries that were once just colored spots on a map. Our understanding of other worlds and other cultures has helped us feel that we are not just citizens of America but citizens of the world. Our family now stretches far beyond America's borders.

I do not know how many guests will join us this Thanksgiving. The number seems to grow each year. But, as we join hands around the table, I will once again reflect that we are also joining hands around the world. We give thanks for all our children, both home-grown and international, who have enriched our lives.

Ruffles and Flourishes

"Why does the turkey have ruffled socks on?" our four-year-old daughter, Eleanor, asked my mother when we spent a Thanksgiving at her house. Mother laughed. "That's so Grandaddy does not get his fingers all greasy when he holds onto the drumsticks to cut them off and slice their meat." She showed Eleanor how to make them. You can, too.

Gently fold an 8.5 x 11-inch piece of white paper in half lengthwise. Measure in 2 inches from where the two edges meet and draw a line with pencil. Have your child make cuts from the folded edge to this line, as close together as possible. The cuts will be 3.5 inches long. Press the folded edge against the palm of your hand to make the paper loops open up a bit. Now tape the ruffle around the end of the drumsticks with masking tape. Want the ruffles to be very full and frilly? Just use two ruffles per drumstick, instead of one.

The First Snow

I t is cold in the bedroom this morning, the kind of chill that makes you pull the covers up over your nose. As we lie in bed in that state somewhere between asleep and awake, I hear the radio crackling with reports of school closings on the other side of the mountains. "Stay tuned for further announcements for counties east of the Blue Ridge," the weatherman warns.

"The children will be so excited," I mumble sleepily to my husband. "They'll probably have a snow day." I mentally begin to plan the party we always have to celebrate the first snowfall.

"The children," Bob laughed, "don't live here anymore."

My mind snapped to attention. Darn, I realized, he was right. We've not had a snow party here for years.

When you live in the south, you sometimes have to wait a long time for snow. Growing up in Illinois, I remember that, by Thanksgiving, our land would have long been covered in a soft blanket of snow. But, in Virginia, the winter's bleakness can drag on and on, the dim afternoons blending too early into night.

As I rise and make my way sleepily to the kitchen, the leaden skies reflect a dreary light, but when I look toward the mountains I can see that gray clouds are already looming above them. I open the door; the air smells blue and cold—like snow.

As I put on the kettle, I hear the deep rumble of the school bus, slowly making its way up the hill. School has not been cancelled here, at least not yet. Perhaps they will have to close the school early if the storm builds. And then, when the school bus brings the neighborhood children home, I will hear that familiar winter sound—the clanking and rattling of tire chains, sounding for all the world like Marley's ghost in a *Christmas Carol*.

Our children's excitement on days like these was matched only by my own. Bob says I am a fool for snow and he is right. I yearn for the brightness of a snow-covered world, the pale winter sun touching the sparkling drifts and making the once-gloomy landscape shimmer. I do not mind bidding farewell to winter's stark landscape. The snow soothes its rawness and brightens the short days. I love the way the sharp skeletons of the trees plump up as snow covers their thin branches and the way the raw brown fields disappear beneath a blanket of white. Snow makes the wait for spring bearable.

The children and I always celebrated the first snowfall with a party. When they were finally tired of filling our yard with snowmen and snow angels, when they'd had their fill of endless snowball fights staged from behind the walls of their snow forts, they would troop in, cheeks rosy and noses red, and gather around the stove with big mugs of cocoa and a bowl of popcorn. For this once-a-year occasion, I would let them toast marshmallows in the woodstove—a messy affair guaranteed to mean much scraping up of gooey glops of dropped sweetness.

Bob comes into the kitchen. "I checked the weather channel. Looks like we're in for a big one," he says, sitting down at the table and wrapping his hands around a steaming cup of coffee. "I'd better bring in some more wood."

"Will the storm make it to the city?" I ask.

"Yup," he says. "It's going to keep moving right up the seaboard toward Boston."

I begin to smile.

"You're thinking of the girls, aren't you?" he asks.

I nod. Our daughters share an apartment in the city. Tomorrow or the next day, their desolate cityscape will be buried in a soft embrace of snow.

I open a cupboard and begin rummaging around.

"What are you looking for?" Bob asks, buttering his toast. "The jam is on the table."

"I'm just looking to see if I have any popcorn," I reply. "And some cocoa."

Bob looks at me quizzically.

"If I find some, I'm going to make Eleanor and Sarah a snow party kit." Way in the back of a cupboard, I discover a half-empty jar of popcorn and a couple of cocoa packets. I grin triumphantly as I plop them down on the counter.

Bob just shakes his head, gives me an amused smile, and kisses me good-bye.

Suddenly, the house begins to make the familiar creakings it always does as it settles in for a storm. A quiet sense of expectancy envelops me as I stand at the door, waving good-bye and watching the storm advancing across the valley. The first flakes start to swirl past the windows.

There is nothing quite like the first snowfall, especially when it is so late in coming and so eagerly anticipated. If I pack up the snow-party fixings and drive into the village quickly, I can get the box in the morning's mail. The girls should have it by tomorrow.

MAKING PAPER SNOWFLAKES

No snow at your house? Let your children decorate your windows with paper snowflakes. Just take a square of paper, fold it in half, and then half again. Cut an arc so that when you unfold the paper, you have a circle. Now, fold the paper in half again along the first fold line and then fold that semicircle into thirds. This way, you'll get a six-pointed snowflake just like the real ones. Then, simply make tiny cuts into the folds and at the edge of the triangle of paper. When you open it up, voilà—you have a snowflake. The more cuts you make, and the smaller they are, the more delicate and realistic your snowflake will be. With practice your children will learn how far into the paper to cut without cutting through, and just how much paper to take out. Although small cuticle scissors with curved blades are perfect for making exquisite snowflakes, they should be used only by older children. Blunt-tipped children's scissors work fine, especially if the paper is thin. (Tissue paper is perfect for learning.) Tape your snowflakes to a window and create your own snowstorm.

Let's Fly a Kite

A strong summer breeze blows our flag almost straight out. Against a backdrop of clear summer sky, the Stars and Stripes flutters and flaps with each gust. My husband comes inside and leans against the door.

"It's a beautiful day to fly a kite," he says, hanging his coat on a peg. "Too bad we don't have one anymore."

"Want to make one?" I ask.

Bob stops short with surprise, then grins. "Sure," he says. "I'll see if we've got any dowels in the workshop."

As Bob heads downstairs, I remember the many kites we've flown over the years. There were colorful box kites and Mylar kites that glistened iridescently in the sunlight. On Father's Day, one year, the children gave Bob a stunt kite that had several strings. By pulling on first one, then another, he could make it dive and swirl, do loop-the-loops and dip and soar.

But of all the kites we've had, the ones I've loved the most were those we made ourselves. They were simple affairs, really. Just two crossed sticks, some string, and some paper. The children decorated them with wonderful designs, painting some to look like dragons with flaming tails, some to resemble birds. Others were decorated with flowers or animals, funny faces, or abstract designs worthy of Picasso.

Sometimes, our homemade kites were a bit wild in flight, so we had to race back inside, find the rag bag, and tear up an old sheet to make tails. At times, Bob would fasten the kites to his fishing rod; the line shrieked through the reel as it ran out, and the children vied for turns to reel the kite in. Bob's fishing-rod arrangement made for some interesting comments from passersby on the beach: Following our upward gaze, they would laugh and often say something like "Looks like you caught a big one there." Such comments inspired the children to make a number of fish kites.

The kids loved sending notes up the kite strings. They would write a wish on a round piece of paper, cut a slit on one side, and slip it on the kite string. The wind, vibrating across the string, would set the note dancing. In slow circles, the note crept its way higher and higher up the string toward the kite until it was out of sight. When we pulled in the kite, the notes were always gone. Our daughter Eleanor decided they must have been snatched by angels.

At the top of a mountain not far from our home sits a cluster of cottages. To live in one of them with their sweeping views of the Blue Ridge Mountains is a coveted prize. The cottages tend to be handed down from friend to friend, many of them graduate students at the local university. Each year, residents of the mountain hold Kite Day.

Some years back, one of my husband's students who lived on the mountain invited us to bring the children and join the festivities. The week before was full of feverish activity as Bob and the children spent every evening down in the workshop, putting the finishing touches on their kites.

The long-awaited day dawned bright and sunny, with a nice strong breeze blowing in from the southwest. We packed a picnic, herded everyone into the station wagon, and headed for the mountain, each child carefully guarding his or her creation on the trip.

Bob helped the kids launch their kites, and then we lay back on a blanket, watching them as they flew their celestial works of art. Each child had a different approach. Drew urged his purple and green dragon higher and higher by running up and down the slope to help it gain altitude. Sarah, our youngest, tugged often at her string, looking back at us for instructions. Every now and then, we saw her move across the grass to help a younger child untangle her string or add more bits of ribbon to a tail. Eleanor stood in one place, carefully playing out the line as her kite soared ever upward. She tipped her head back and studied the pattern that her bird-kite made against the sky and stayed on the hill long after most of the other children had tired of the sport. As families began to gather for the evening picnic, Eleanor let her kite go. By the time she reached our blanket, it was only a tiny speck in the pale blue sky.

The children had made the kites; they were theirs to do with as they wished. Nonetheless, we were surprised. "Why did you let it go?" I asked her.

She simply replied, "Because it wanted to be free."

A few years ago, when my friend Susan learned that Eleanor was going to a recently war-torn country in Africa to direct a project that would help rebuild schools and roads, bridges and hospitals, she asked, "How can you let her go to such a dangerous place?"

Let was not the right word, I replied. Eleanor was twenty-six; I had not told her what to do since she'd finished school. By the age of twenty-one, decisions about our children's lives were theirs, not ours. What I did not tell Susan was that, like notes on a kite string, I had said many a prayer for Eleanor's safety, hoping that a guardian angel would watch over her.

Recently, after Eleanor was evacuated from that same African country when war suddenly resumed, I remembered Susan's questioning my ability to let my daughter go to a war zone. "You see," I could almost hear her say, "even the government wants to call her back home." And she did come back , but it was only for a while. Now, she's off again.

Yet I knew that I had "let her go" years earlier. Is that not, after all, the goal of being a parent? We can only hope that when we finally let go of the string, our children will be happy and free, strong enough to weather any storm.

On that Kite Day so many years ago, when Eleanor let her kite go, we knew that she would one day soar high and true on her own. And she has.

Up, Up, and Away

Generally believed to have first been flown in China more than 2,000 years ago, kites today come in all sizes and shapes and with many different purposes. Creating one is a simple matter. Try making one yourself out of paper, adhesive tape, and some wooden barbecue skewers or dowels. Your local library undoubtedly has books on how to make kites. If you desire something a little more sophisticated, there are a variety of websites that will tell you how to make dozens of different kites and provide more information about kites than you ever dreamed existed.

Cutting Down the Oak

O ne night, three summers ago, a wild wind whipped round our house. It whistled at the windows and howled down the chimney. Rain hammered on the roof all night; sleep was difficult. In the morning, the light in the kitchen seemed oddly strange—brighter than usual at breakfast time. When I opened the back door, I saw a great deal more sky than usual. As I tried to decipher this in my sleepy confusion, I suddenly realized that a gigantic piece of the oak tree was lying on the ground. The gnarled branches of the fallen limb reached up as though beseeching to be pulled back into place. I stood staring in shock and disbelief. Then, wrapping a sweater around my shoulders against the early-morning chill, I ran across the wet grass and leaned against the tree's massive trunk. As I gazed up at the splintered remains of the huge branch, two squirrels ran back and forth, frantically trying to get their bearings. I stared at the raw, yellow wound in disbelief and wondered if the rest of the tree could be saved.

When I called our tree man, John Stokes, he came right over. John is a soft-spoken man who loves trees as much as I do. We agree that they have souls and consider them guardians of the small communities of birds and bugs and other creatures who live in them. We shared the secret notion that trees are more important than houses. When we bought this place, my husband told my parents, "Faith has bought some trees. A house goes with them."

Bob came out to join John and me as we silently walked around the oak and clambered over the jumble of downed branches. John shook his head sadly and examined the standing half of the tree. "See that rot?" he said, pointing to a dark stain. We nodded. "Water has seeped into the crotch. I don't know how deep the decay goes."

He climbed around in the tree, tapping and knocking. Then he cabled together the two remaining limbs and gave the roots a deep feeding. Just before he left, he placed his hand on the tree for a silent moment. It looked as though he were giving it a blessing. The next day, he removed the fallen branches.

That autumn, the squirrels gathered acorns and buried them in their usual hiding places. When the children came to visit, we spread blankets beneath the remaining half of the tree, where we were shaded from the late afternoon sun by its generous leaves. As we sat beneath the broad, spreading branches, we recalled the tree fort that Drew and his buddies had built in the crotch of the tree. "No girls allowed," his sign declared. We laughed as we realized that his two daughters would someday erect a sign that might state quite the opposite. We recalled the many tea parties that were held beneath the tree's branches, tea parties that were made even more charming by the tiny acorn-cap cups that Eleanor and Sarah made for their dolls. Bob suspended a swing from a low branch. A woven hammock hung from the tree, inviting us to rest awhile, read a book, and look at the clouds.

The tree had always been a focus for family activities. Birthday parties were held at a table set beneath its branches. It was the base for games of capture the flag, kick the can, and beckons wanted. Each fall we delighted in watching the blue jays and tufted titmice, cardinals and chickadees dart and flit among the branches, then swoop down to pluck a sunflower seed from the feeder I had suspended from a branch. The family of squirrels who made their home in the oak delighted us with their acrobatics as they slid down the wire to the feeder to steal seeds.

Sarah played house beneath the tree and later wrote poetry there. Eleanor climbed as high as she could and looked off into the distance where she was sure her future lay. Drew practiced belaying from the top of the tree to the ground in one swift movement—one that he would repeat eight years later on the cliffs in Yellowstone Park.

The spring after the storm, the oak thrived, and we gradually got used to its lopsided look. But that was also the year of a summer-long drought, and the leaves turned brown in August rather than the usual October. John Stokes paid monthly house calls and merely said, "We'll see." The next winter was bitter cold, with little snow to provide much-needed moisture.

I had always used the size of the tree's leaves as a guide for planting: big as a mouse's ear, I would plant the corn; big as a squirrel's ear, the tomatoes could be put out and the melon and cucumber seeds could go in. But two years after the storm, the leaves were still struggling by June. John came out to visit his patient. "If the leaves don't grow, you're going to get sun scald," he said. "The drought and the rot have obviously taken their toll." Looking at my stricken face he added, "But I've seen trees worse off than this make it. Let's just wait and see. Perhaps we will have a good summer."

But we didn't. And the following winter, a strong north wind cracked one of the remaining major limbs in two. Last spring, the oak did not leaf out. While the maples blossomed with red, fuzzy catkins and the willows turned pale chartreuse, the oak remained cloaked in winter's bareness. The other trees were full of life: Birds twittered in the branches, squirrels scampered about, spring breezes rustled the new leaves. But the oak tree stood silent.

John came to see his patient one last time. As we stood quietly looking at the oak, he removed his hat.

The next morning, the air was full of the whine of the chainsaw and the drone of the wood chipper. I hid myself in my study and turned the music up loud. By noon, the yard was still. The oak was gone. Although we had grown used to the gradually diminishing shade cast by our poor, old tree, the harsh sunlight on the lawn was hard on my eyes.

John pointed proudly to an enormous stack of firewood. "There's enough here to keep you warm all winter," he said. I smiled. It would be a cozy legacy from a dear friend. Then he showed me a huge pile of wood chip mulch. It cheered me to realize that the death of the oak would mean renewed life for the azaleas and rhododendrons.

When my husband came home that evening, we walked up to where the oak had been. Bob tried to comfort me by observing that the view of our neighbor's fields was now unobstructed. He pointed to a strong, young maple sapling that stood at the edge of the woods. "Maples grow quickly and their colors are beautiful in the autumn," he said. "I think it would be good for you—for all of us—if we were to move that tree here." And so we did.

Bob was right. When something or someone we love disappears it creates an empty space, a hole in the fabric of our lives. I think it is our nature to want to fill the void. Whenever a person I love has died, I have planted a tree in their memory. A dogwood for my friend Susie, a stewartia for my mother, golden rain trees for a neighbor's son, Brian, and for my father. As the trees have flourished, my sorrow has diminished. Those trees will be here long after I have departed.

The oak tree sheltered our family; it protected our house from winter winds and gave us shade in the summer. But as I look at the little maple, I realize that, in a few years, it will gracefully accept the mantle inherited from its predecessor. Our grandchildren will build a tree house in it. Bob and I will read in its cooling shade. Each spring when its bright, red catkins blossom forth, it will remind me that Nature replaces that which she takes away and that a tree in new leaf is a sure sign of hope.

Camping Out

As I sit on a log, pale aspen leaves above me flutter in the late-afternoon breeze like bits of silver foil. My family has gone downstream to fish. Our granddaughters have promised to catch us dinner. I'm thawing some hamburger, just in case.

We've been camping alongside this stream in Wyoming for two days now. As soon as we arrived, the children began our campsite ritual. How quickly they made our private piece of wilderness into a home. The soap is in its little mesh bag tied to a gallon jug of handwashing water; the mirror hangs from a branch close by; the campstools are neatly placed around a fire ring. The kids have gathered enough driftwood and downed branches for a week's worth of fires, although we only plan a three-night stay. Propped up against a tree are two perfect hot dog– and marshmallow-roasting sticks that they found at our first stop, 500 miles ago.

Our granddaughters, Carter and Mason, have created a striking centerpiece from tall spires of magenta fireweed and some pale pink lupines. Flat blossoms of white yarrow contrast with the delicate flowers of purple monkshood. On the table they have spread the red-and-white-checked oilcloth that we usually use on our porch table.

Behind me in the woods, I hear the scrunch of tires on gravel. Is it an RV or a car full of tenters? I let my ears do the detective work for me.

The click of doors opening unleashes a babble of children's voices. After a moment I sort out the voices of two young children, a mother, and a father.

Over the happy din, I can make out a mother organizing the troops. The flump of a tent on soft ground is followed by the unmistakable hollow clang of aluminum tent poles tumbling out of their sack onto pine needles. Soon the woods echo with the sharp tapping of a hammer against metal tent stakes.

I swivel slowly on my log and quietly observe the tent raising. Each child holds an aluminum pole upright while Dad pounds in the stakes that hold the guy lines. The two young voices belong to two little boys. Both appear to be about ten. One has a crew cut; the other has a mop of black curls.

Once their tent has been set up to their liking, the two little boys set out to investigate the campground. Like puppies sniffing the air, they make ever-widening circles into the surrounding woods. Their third pass brings them close to my log. They stop. Two pair of brown eyes regard me solemnly.

"Hi," I say.

"Hi," they reply.

"I'm from Virginia. How about you?"

"I'm Matt," the taller child offers. "Me and my family are from New Jersey. This is my friend Hector. He spends summers with us."

Eager to get a word in, Hector adds, "Yeah. This is my third year with the Pelowskis. I'm from New York City."

"Big place," I respond.

"Yes, but not as big as this," he says, sweeping his arms to take in the towering spruce and the Grand Tetons in the distance. "At home, I can't see the stars."

Compared to the canyons of New York, this is a vast landscape. "You're right, Hector," I concur. "There's a lot of sky out here. Tell me where else you've been."

They need no encouragement. The two are like a stand-up act. One starts, the other finishes as they recite each of their trip's stops: Grand Old Opry, the Badlands, Mount Rushmore.

"You've camped out a lot?" I ask the boys.

They look at each other. "Sort of," Matt says slowly.

"This trip is the first time I've been out of New Jersey... or New York," says Hector. "It took me a couple years to be able to sleep outside. But last summer, me and Matt, we slept in the tent in his backyard for two nights." He looks proud at having achieved such a feat.

Matt joins in, "Then we all went to the beach for a week. Cape May, New Jersey. Ya' know it?"

I nod.

"I'd never seen a real ocean before. Just the East River," Hector admits. "So this year, Dick—that's Mr. Pelowski—said that since I'd seen one ocean, I should see the other," he continues.

"Right," Matt says, having remained silent long enough. "None of us has seen the Pacific."

"In a week, we're gonna be there," both boys shout in unison, slapping high fives.

I smile at the boys' obvious excitement and wish them a good journey as they leave to continue their explorations. Camping out, I decide, is a state of mind, the challenge of the new. It's where you take a few essentials of life and head for uncharted territory. It does not necessarily have to be wilderness. It does not even have to involve travel.

Hector's obvious pride in conquering the strangeness of sleeping in a tent reminds me of the year our son first went to summer camp. He decided he needed to practice.

The first night, I tucked him in under the dining-room table. We'd thrown two old blankets over the top and left the light on all night long. After two nights spent there, he said he was ready to move to the tent we'd set up out in the backyard. But he took his little sister for company. Both of them had flashlights. They came back in by ten the first night; around midnight on the second. On the third night, Drew said Eleanor could sleep inside. Now, thirty years later, Drew is a mountaineer and sometimes sleeps in a sling fastened to a sheer rock face by two steel pins. We conquer our fears one step at a time.

I rise from my log and walk down to the bank of the stream. Camping out, if we answer the challenge, makes us reach beyond what we think we can really do. At first, it is good to have a flashlight. Later, we can turn it off.

I spot my family walking toward me on the other side of the stream. Carter is in the lead. Time was, she was terrified of worms. Now she baits her own hooks. She and Mason spot me and proudly wave six trout in the air. I guess we'll save the hamburgers for tomorrow.

Nature's Tic-Tac-Toe

After a long day spent hiking or fishing, children sometimes need a quiet game to play. Try creating a "game board" for tic-tac-toe on a spot of bare earth. With a stick draw the game's lines. The opponents can draw their X's and O's with the same stick. Or be creative: Try dark stones and light stones, or pebbles and leaves. Our daughters delighted in searching out perfectly round stones for the O's and creating little X's out of crossed twigs.

Section III
AS A GRANDMOTHER

Children are the hands by which we take hold of heaven.

Henry Ward Beecher

The Christening Gown

S everal months ago, our son, Drew, called. "Hi Mom," he said. "You're going to be a grandmother again."

Although I had been anticipating the news for some time, I was not prepared for the tears that suddenly filled my eyes. As I hung up the phone and told my husband the news, he grabbed me, and we danced around the kitchen, whooping with laughter. When we caught our breath, Bob said, "Looks like the christening gown will be worn again."

I nodded and looked back a few years to when our first grandchild, Carter Elisabeth, was born. The first thing I did when I learned of her impending arrival was to find the family christening gown. I had not seen it in nearly twenty-five years.

As I climbed the stairs to the attic, I remembered how carefully I had packed the gown away after the christening of our last baby. I had wondered then how many years would pass before I would get it out again.

I found the box lying in a dim corner. Carefully untying the ribbons that fastened the lid, I unfolded the tissue paper and caressed the soft, creamy folds of silk.

The gown is so old that its once-sparkling whiteness has softened to a pale ivory. The narrow hand-sewn seams are carefully rolled so that no rough stitching will ever touch a baby's soft skin. Delicate handmade lace edges the little collar and sleeves, and rows of little tucks have accommodated babies both large and small. The gown has been worn both by tiny newborns and strapping one-year-olds; it has been taken in and let out many times.

Five generations of Bedfords have worn this gown and its matching silk coat and bonnet. The initials of each child and his or her birthdate have been carefully embroidered in the lining—some more skillfully than others.

"I don't know how to embroider!" I confessed to my grandmother as my firstborn's christening day approached.

"Here, dear, I'll show you," she patiently replied as she set me to work practicing on a bit of muslin. The thread broke, knots formed, letters straggled.

"Won't you please do it?" I begged.

She simply shook her head. "It's a mother's privilege," she said.

After a week of practice, I finally felt up to the task and carefully embroidered W.A.B. 8-2-1964. Grandmother was proud of me.

As I lifted the dress and looked at my handiwork, I was, too. With each child, I'd grown more proficient. Drew's initials had been done in tiny cross-stitch; Eleanor's were in block; Sarah's flowed in curlicues. I ran my fingers up the long row of initials and dates until I reached the first set: N.P.B. 1-4-1863.

Packed into the box with the christening gown is a little pouch containing photographs of almost all the babies who have worn this dress. I unfolded the faded velvet case that holds the daguerreotype of the first baby to wear the gown. Nathan Peter rests in the arms of Grandmother Lovelace, looking very serious indeed. He was christened in Lauderdale County, Tennessee, on the eve of the Civil War. Grant marched near the Bedford farm later on but left the homestead untouched.

In the next picture I see Nathan Peter as a proud father. He is holding his infant son, Nathaniel Lynn, who pulls at the ribbons of the bonnet. Standing behind her husband is Katie Lynn Robert Bedford. In less than a year she would be a widow and return to the home of her father, a doctor, whose grandfather had fled France to help found the Huguenot Church in South Carolina. Little Nathaniel was raised by four widows: his mother, his grandmother, and two aunts—not an uncommon household for the post–Civil War South. No wonder he ran away from home at fourteen to become a cabin boy on a ship bound from Savannah. Twenty years later, however, he looks quite the respectable businessman as he poses with his son, Nathaniel Forrest, outside a church in Jacksonville, Florida. Little Nathaniel plays with the flower pinned to his father's lapel. Nathaniel's mother came to America from a tiny European country that has now disappeared from the maps. She did not believe in banks, preferring instead to invest in jewelry. One of her rings was given to me when I married her grandson.

My husband was the next baby to wear the christening dress. A Yankee by accident, he was born in Boston when the Army sent his father there to attend radar school at M.I.T. during the Second World War. The little family was soon posted to Hobe Sound, Florida, so, as his Georgian grandfather was fond of saying, at least Bob was christened in the South. In the photograph, Bob is asleep in his mother's arms while his father, dressed in his captain's uniform, looks on proudly. After the war ended and Bob's father returned from the Pacific, the little family grew quickly. Bob soon had three sisters. Although they all wore the christening gown, not all of their pictures are in the envelope. As Bob's mother says, "When you have four children, some things get forgotten."

Our own children's christenings marked new chapters in our marriage, for each was born in a different city. The happy memories of every new home are captured in the photographs of our babies' christenings.

The christening gown has traveled with each generation, first by flatboat, later by horse and wagon, then by steamship, automobile, and truck. For Carter, it made its first trip by plane. The previous wearers had all been Eastern babies, but for Carter's christening, the little dress traveled to the mountains of Utah.

I carefully mended a seam and checked the stitching on the tiny pearl buttons, then I folded it gently back into its box. Smoothing the soft silk in place was like touching a butterfly's wing. It is delicate but enduring. Despite more than a century of christenings, the precious heirloom looks as though it could be worn for a century more.

As I walked to the village to mail the gown, I pondered my new role. For thirty years I had worn many hats: wife and mother, farmer and writer. I realized that I would soon have a new hat to wear—a grandmother's hat.

Carter had not even arrived yet, but already I felt venerable, as though a mantle of wisdom had been gently placed upon my shoulders.

At the post office, I met an old friend, Guy, who had been a grandfather for at least a dozen years. As we stood in line, I told him the good news of the soon-to-be birth of our first grandchild. I confessed to being a bit nervous in the new role and asked him what being a grandparent truly means. "A grandparent," he told me solemnly, "is someone who tells the stories."

"Well then, here, Sonja," I said as I pushed my package across the counter to our postmistress clerk. "Send this off to Drew and Jill. It will be the first chapter of the old stories."

Soon the christening gown will be worn again by the latest addition to the newest generation. Sitting on the porch, sipping tea, Bob and I wonder out loud how many more times it will be worn by our grandchildren. Where else will it travel? Will we live to see it worn by our great-grandchildren?

I smile. The answers to those questions will be part of the new stories. I look forward to telling them.

A Simple Christening Bonnet

To make a christening bonnet for a baby (or a doll):

1. *Take a small, square, lace-edged handkerchief and fold it in half. (If you have an heirloom handkerchief, perhaps one carried at a wedding or owned by a grandfather, so much the better.)*

2. *Sew two of the short edges together. This seam will run down the back of the baby's head from the crown of the head to the nape of the neck.*

3. *Try the bonnet on the baby and fold back the unjoined edges, or front of the bonnet, to just in front of the baby's ears. If the handkerchief is too large, you may need to make tucks in this front fold, so that it extends back only about one-third of the way onto the body of the bonnet. Tack this fold in place.*

4. *Cut two lengths of white satin ribbon about 12 inches long, fold the raw edges under, and sew them to the bottom front corners of the fold.*

5. *Place the bonnet on the baby and tie the ribbons gently beneath the chin. And remember to take a picture and save it for the baby's grandchildren!*

A Walk with a Child

My granddaughter, Carter, and I are going for a hike. I've loaded my pack with some crackers and some grapes, lemonade, and a diaper.

When Carter's father was a boy, we took many family hikes—through the rain forests of Washington's Olympic peninsula, up the White Mountains of New Hampshire, among the valleys of the Blue Ridge Mountains. The family photo albums are full of pictures of Drew and his sisters carving special walking sticks, posing in the gnarled roots of gigantic trees, or terrifying me by hanging over sheer cliffs. But it's been a long time since I took a hike with a two-year-old.

I figure, in an afternoon, we can go a mile or two, perhaps from Carter's house to the first meadow and back. The trails here in the mountains of Utah can be steep. I know that on the way home, I may have to carry her piggyback for a bit. This thought makes me extra glad that Drew and Jill did not wait any longer to have children. Were I ten or fifteen years older, hoisting a grandchild up on my back might be out of the question.

As we near the trail, my eyes take in the lovely woods, the colorful wildflowers, the dramatic rock outcroppings. But we've a hike to do, so I don't dally. Carter leads the way with a little step that makes her look like a frisky colt, sort of a cross between a gallop and a skip.

"Good," I think. "This is a fine pace. We'll make good time."

Suddenly Carter hunkers down in the trail. "A stick, Gammy," she says, picking it up. She discovers another one and declares, "Two sticks." She places them in my hand for my inspection.

"Very pretty," I say, taking the little sticks and putting them in my pocket. Then I take her hand and lead her onward. "Here we go."

We walk hand in hand for two or three minutes until a flash of red catches Carter's eye. "Ooooo, pretty," she says and darts off the trail. Caught in the light of a sunbeam, a bright-red clump of cardinal flowers glows in the shadows of the forest. I follow and find her stroking the delicate blossoms. She looks up at me tentatively.

"Pick it?" she asks.

"Just one," I say. "We want to leave some for other people to see."

Carter solemnly picks one tiny bloom and lays it gently in my hand. "Is booful," she says, and I nod in agreement. I put it in my pocket with the sticks.

A few hundred feet further we come upon a pile of boulders that had fallen from the cliffs high above. Of course they must be climbed.

As I hover behind Carter, hands ready to catch her, my mind drifts back thirty years as I remember watching her father climb the jungle gyms in New York's Central Park. Our first apartment was in an old brownstone on the East Side. The walk to the park was lined with brick stoops. Drew knew every one of them; they were his Himalayas. Each low wall had to be climbed. Every phone booth became a play-house. Fruit stands needed investigating (and an apple was invariably bought). Stoplights were carefully watched for the green. "OK, Mommy. Go!" Drew would shout as he galloped across the intersection, pulling me behind him.

A rock teeters beneath Carter's foot and I dart to catch her, but she regains her balance and climbs higher. The rhythm of living with little people seeps slowly back into my consciousness. Trust in their abilities. Bumps and falls teach them lessons my warnings never can. It's coming back to me now.

Drew moved to Utah so that he could ski steep slopes and climb tall mountains. Clearly, Carter is following in his footsteps. When she has carefully climbed down, we sit on a rock and share the crackers and lemonade. She gathers a few of the smaller stones and asks, "Pudit inna pocket?" I gladly oblige.

As we continue our hike (walk? amble?) I remember, too, that a walk with a child is about process, not completion. The goal of the meadow was mine, not Carter's. I slow down and let her set the pace.

By the side of the trail she spots a butterfly. I had not seen it. When you are less than three feet from the ground, you notice a great deal that we taller folk do not. The butterfly is dead, its bright markings dulled, its wings tattered. Carter holds it tenderly in her hand and strokes its furry body. Together we marvel at the colors of its wings.

She throws it up in the air and orders, "Fly." But it drifts slowly back to earth. She carefully picks it up and gives it to me. It joins the other treasures in my pocket. I am beginning to feel like a walking Museum of Natural History.

A bit farther on, we see a line of ants marching across the trail. Carter is fascinated and flops down on the moist earth to inspect them. I hesitate, then realize that our clothes are washable and so are we. I lie down beside her. From this vantage point, the ants take on a whole new identity. They are not just tiny black spots but earnest workers on a mission. They pass one other, antennae waving, each one locked into her special job. Not for them a side trip to smell a flower or explore a hollow log.

I place a twig in the ants' path to see what they will do. Without missing a beat, they climb right over it. Carter follows my lead and places a tiny pebble in a small break in the stream of ants. They climb over that, too. We add ever-bigger pebbles until finally we place one that is too large for the ants to climb. Their purposeful parade divides and flows around it. I tell Carter how they lay down a scent trail so they can find their way home and that, when they wiggle their antennae, it's like talking. How much of this she understands I don't know, but she lies quietly and listens as she watches the ants intently.

Carter sits up slowly and rubs her eyes. "Go home now?" she asks. "See Mommy?" Ah, yes, I remember. When one is sleepy, home is best.

For the past few months, when someone asked her, "How old are you?" Carter has been replying, "I pushin' two." Tomorrow is her birthday; we are visiting for the festivities. Part of my reason for this outing with Carter is so that Jill can put up decorations and bake the birthday cake.

We start back down the trail, more slowly this time. We never did get to the meadow. As a matter of fact, we've probably gone no more than half a mile. But my pockets are bulging, and we've seen many new things.

I make a mental note that, next time, I shall tuck into my pack a magnifying glass and a small cushion for me to sit on while Carter digs holes in the dirt with a stick.

Carter begins to fret, so I move my pack around to the front and swing her up on my back. A tired little head bobbles against my shoulder. As I slow my pace, I notice a lovely patch of light green lichen with frilly edges. It looks like a celadon pillow edged in crochet. In my usual power-walk mode, I might have missed it.

To walk with a child, I have remembered, is not about "getting there." It is about discoveries . . . and rediscoveries.

"Thank you, Carter," I say softly.

"Tankooo" echoes a sleepy, little voice.

The shadows lengthen on the path. In the distance, I can see Carter's house. Birthday balloons are already bobbing brightly on the mailbox. Jill has put her afternoon to good use. Then again, so have I.

HIKING WITH CHILDREN

Few things are more delightful than a walk with a child, especially when you pre-pare for your adventure in advance. Here are a few items to bear in mind before you hit the trail.

Consider the weather when you pack your knapsack. A poncho might be in order, as well as a sun hat and windbreaker.

Be sure to include sunscreen and bug repellent and a few bandages for the inevitable scraped knee.

Take plenty of water (far more thirst quenching than juices) and some high-energy snacks. Our children used to love to help us make "gorp"—a trail mix made up of unsalted peanuts, raisins, granola, and chocolate (or carob) chips.

A flashlight is not only handy for emergencies; it is also wonderful for peering into caves or dark recesses in the roots of trees. Include a magnifying glass for closely inspecting creatures and flowers, and plastic bags for bringing home treasures.

Little ones love to have a tiny pack of their own and feel quite grown-up if they can carry some of the important things like a small compass, a whistle, and pencil and paper for making "scientific" notes or maps. Be sure not to make their packs too heavy; depending on age, children should be able to carry a jacket and their own little water bottle.

A hiking stick is a fun addition to any hike and can usually be picked up along the trail. Our children loved to use a rest break to personalize their sticks, peeling off the bark and making designs in the wood with a pointed rock.

Plan ahead for emergencies. For safety's sake, let someone know the route of your planned hike and your estimated time of return.

Be realistic in your goals, rest often, and let the child set the pace. Remember, a walk with a little one is not necessarily about reaching a destination; it is about spending time together.

Two Hands Clapping

Although I had often heard that you do not miss something until it is gone, I did not truly understand the truth behind the adage. Then, last month, I lost the use of my right hand and was astonished at how much I needed it.

Carpal tunnel syndrome is something of an occupational hazard among writers. When I noticed numbness, weakness, and a deep ache in my hand, I began to worry. When holding a pen became excruciating, I panicked.

"This will keep your fingers from moving," the doctor said as she fitted a strapped contraption onto my right hand. "You may not use this hand at all for three weeks," she added, pressing the last strap in place. "Then, we will see."

"May I take it off to sleep?" I asked; visions of insomnia loomed before me.

"Only for bathing," she answered.

"But I'm a writer," I moaned.

"Use the other hand," she said crisply.

It wasn't until dinner that evening (my husband cooked; I acted as a one-handed sous chef) that the full enormity of this dilemma hit me. Bob and I had been discussing the impending arrival of our second grandchild when I suddenly remembered my promise to help after the baby came.

"What if my hand isn't better?" I fretted. "What if I still have to wear this stupid brace?" I dropped my immobilized arm on the table with a loud clunk.

"You can be plenty of help with your left hand," Bob said, smiling encouragingly.

True, I could probably manage some simple meals. I could push the vacuum and mop with my left hand. I could even drive; I'd done that on the way home from the doctor's office. But I'd hoped to take full care of our first grandchild, Carter, so that Jill could rest and attend to the needs of the new baby.

Perhaps Carter would have mastered the art of dressing herself by the time I arrived. She had been working on buttons during our last visit; I certainly couldn't help her with that now.

"But how will I do Carter's braids?" I wondered out loud to Bob.

"Don't worry," he assured me. "She will think having a robotic grandmother is cool." I threatened to bop him with my brace.

"And how will I play finger games?" I groaned.

Bob looked up quizzically.

"You know," I said. " 'Here Sits the Lord Mayor' and 'Two Little Men'? And whoever sang, 'I'm a Little Tea Pot' with an aluminum and Velcro spout?"

Bob nodded in sober agreement.

One of the delights of being a grandmother, I've discovered, has been rediscovering all the little games I played with my own children. Each time we visit Carter, I remember more. Like bubbles rising slowly to the surface of my memory, songs and riddles, finger games and crafts burst into my consciousness. Just like riding a bicycle, one never forgets how to balance a child on one's knee and bobbling her gently, sing, "This is the way the Lady rides, trot, trot, trot." Certainly, the art of making a fort from sofa pillows and blankets is not easily forgotten.

I hadn't sung "Itsy, Bitsy Spider" for years, but the words came right back. But, with my immobilized hand, I would only be able to make half a spider to crawl up the waterspout. Nor would I be able to fold my hands together to make the steepled church with its wiggly-finger congregation that always sends Carter into fits of giggles. And forget about making silly pictures.

"Draw me a horsie, Gammy, " Carter orders with the imperious tone that is born of knowing that, for now at least, her word is my command. I draw a horse and, at the last moment, give him an elephant's trunk.

"No, that's not right," she squeals.

"Oh?" I say in mock surprise. "Is this better?" I ask, drawing duck feet on the horse.

"No!" She giggles.

"How about now?" I ask, putting horns on the horse's head.

Carter hugs me around the neck and says, "Silly Gammy."

But I cannot even make a straight line with my left hand, so silly pictures are out of the question. Finger painting might work, though. Clumsy as I am with my left hand, I might still be able to make the little finger-paint squiggles that create a reasonable approximation of a picture.

I like to bring Carter a surprise each time we visit, something we can do together. Often it is a book that we can read at bedtime. Sometimes it is a game. Last time, I brought a recipe for edible finger paint. We'd painted and licked our fingers. Carter's dogs, Beaner and Sibby, licked our paintings.

As I showed Carter the finger-paint designs you can make with your hands, I could almost hear Mrs. Miller, my second-grade art teacher, saying, "Now children, if you lay the side of your hand on the paper and wiggle your little finger back and forth it will make a fish."

I showed Carter that one and she named the fish in our picture 'Toot' and 'Puddle,' the names of her two goldfish. We made snaky, vertical movements that looked just like underwater plants. Our fingers and thumbs bunched tightly together made little five-petaled sea flowers, and a line of dots, made by our pinky fingers, created bubbles rising from the fishes' mouths.

For three weeks I followed all the doctor's orders. I wrote stories on my computer, picking out the words with the fingers of my left hand. I achieved a speed of about ten words a minute, but my right hand still had no strength.

"Sometimes these things take more time than we expect," the doctor said. "Come back and see me next week."

But the baby was due soon. We called our son that evening.

"No signs of imminent arrival," Drew said. "Although Jill would be delighted if it were tomorrow."

"Tell that baby to wait a bit longer," I sighed.

"Take vitamin-B complex," suggested my friend, Shirley, who had had carpal tunnel syndrome three years ago.

I faithfully popped two maroon pills morning and night, but the ache continued. At my next visit to the doctor, she mentioned surgery. Seeing my pale face she hurriedly assured me that this would be a last resort.

As I slumped my way out through the doctor's waiting room, I passed two people in wheelchairs and a woman who was almost completely immobilized by an upper-body cast. Suddenly I felt ashamed of my self-pity, realizing that my handicap was minor and, hopefully, temporary.

Three days later the phone rang at three a.m. I fumbled for it in the dark, banging my brace against the headboard. "It's a girl!" Drew announced happily. "Mason Hannah is her name, and she's beautiful."

"Of course she is," I said, rolling over and nudging Bob awake. We listened sleepily to all the details.

I made my plane reservation the next morning, doubled my vitamin-B intake, and prayed for recovery. We got daily updates on the baby's progress: nursing well, gaining weight, sleeping soundly, doing wonderfully. I wished the same could be said of my hand. When Drew corralled Carter long enough to get her to speak on the phone, she shouted, "I'm a big thither, Gammy."

I told her that was a wonderful thing to be and promised to see her very shortly.

"Thee you thoon," said Drew, taking the phone from Carter and doing a good imitation of her lisp.

Perhaps my hand just needed a deadline. Four days before my flight, I noticed that it no longer ached. I was able to pick up light objects. The doctor put me through a few exercises and smiled. "I think you may have recovered," she said.

I breathed a sigh of relief. "But don't rush things, " she cautioned quickly. "I want you to continue to wear the brace at night and do no heavy work with that hand."

"Is finger painting OK?" I asked.

She looked puzzled, then nodded. "That's fine."

Carter greeted me at the door with a big hug. "I'm almost free," she declared, holding up three fingers. Her birthday was in two weeks.

"Well, I'm totally free," I said, slowly rotating my finally unbound hand.

"Silly Gammy," she said. "You're not free; you're big!"

My hand worked just fine. It poured tea for tea parties and diapered Mason; it played dolls and made dinners; it swept the floor . . . gently. As I quietly rocked Mason, while Jill read Carter a story about

King Midas, I realized that all the money in the world cannot buy wholeness or guarantee a sound mind and body. I once saw a T-shirt in a shop window that said "You can never be too rich or too thin." I disagreed with the message when I saw it, for there are certainly problems with both. But, as I cradled Mason with my good hand, I realized that I disagreed with it even more now. I thought about how much we take good health for granted and how much we miss it when it is gone. And without it, nothing else matters.

On our last morning together, Carter wanted to sing the finger song. I began to sing,

"Where is Thumbkin? Where is . . . ?"

"No," she said. "Make their faces."

"Please?" I suggested.

"Please, Gammy," she corrected herself.

So I got out a pen and drew faces on her fingers and mine. Thumbkin and Pointer, Tall Man and Ring Man, and, of course, Pinky—each with two eyes and a smile.

"How are you this morning?" my Pointer bowed to Carter's.

"Very well, I thank you," she sang in return. "Run and hide, run and hide." And our fingers disappeared behind our backs.

Drew called upstairs that it was time to leave for the airport. As I climbed into the car, I turned and called good-bye. Carter waved; five little happy faces flickered on her fingertips. I waved my happy fingers right back.

Finger Lickin' Good

There's nothing a child likes better than to make a wonderful mess. If it is edible, so much the better. Try your hand at making edible finger paint and see if it isn't tops on your children's list of fun things to do.

Buy a package of regular, cook-in-a-pot pudding. White chocolate is best since it can be easily colored. Follow the recipe but reduce the liquid by one-fourth. Remember, you want your "paint" to be thick. Pour the pudding into four bowls and add plenty of food coloring to make brilliant red, sunny yellow, sky blue, and gorgeous green. Put the bowls in the refrigerator until the pudding has cooled.

Now, lay a sheet of finger-paint paper on a washable surface, put a smock on your child, and get out your pudding paints. Let the artist dip great glops of paint out of the bowls and onto the paper. Show them a few fun movements (the sides of their hands can become fish; flowers can be made with the ends of their fingers) and then let them use their imaginations. They'll discover that yellow and red make orange, that blue and yellow make green, and that everything eventually turns into brown. But it's the doing it that's fun. Try it yourself. Pudding paint is wonderfully slippery and squishy. You can let the paintings dry (they will . . . eventually) and hang them up on the refrigerator. But the best part is licking off your fingers.

Gone Fishin'

It has become a tradition that, when Bob and I visit our son and his family, we always take our granddaughter, Carter, fishing. Today's the day.

Our car winds through sagebrush flats that lie on the land like a worn and tattered blanket at the foot of Utah's Wasatch Range. We watch carefully for the fish-shaped sign that reads: FUN FAMILY FISHING. NO LICENSE REQUIRED.

Soon we spy a cabin adorned with a large plaque: GRANDPA'S L'IL FISHING BUDDIES. Hanging from it are thirteen little wooden fish, each emblazoned with the name of a grandchild.

Granpa Gary Rice has been running his trout farm for the past thirty years. Gary's kids loved to fish. He figured others would, too.

He was right. Under a large willow tree festooned with hand-carved ornaments of aquatic creatures, Gary is busy cleaning two fish for a rather squeamish-looking young mother while her twin boys declare, "We're gonna eat 'em for supper."

Gary smiles. "Mighty fine dinner," he affirms.

Carter is fascinated by the jars of fish bait that other children are rolling into little balls and putting on their hooks. She likes the kind that is bright pink with sparkles. But we brought our secret formula: cheese cubes. Bob baits Carter's hook, casts the rod, and hands it to her. Wearing a look of serious concentration, she slowly reels in the line. Nothing. Next time she casts it herself. Suddenly, she feels a tug and squeals, "I've got one, Granbob."

The fish sways on the end of her rod as she parades over to Gary. He dutifully measures it. "Fourteen inches, young lady," he says. "That's quite a whopper." Carter grins with pride. Gary pops the fish into a plastic bag, deftly ties the top, and hands it to the proud fisherman. Carter marches triumphantly back to the car, swinging the bag.

Now, the deal Carter and Bob have is: Once she has landed a fish, he gets to catch one, too. But not here, and not before we've had some lunch.

The last place to eat before you enter the Wasatch National Forest is Kamas, a little ranching town, population 2,100. Judging from the large number of tractor trailers and sheriffs' cars in front of the Kamas Kafe, there has either just been a robbery or the food is pretty tasty. We decide to check it out.

Beneath a large HOME COOKIN sign, twelve red-vinyl stools hug a yellow wooden counter. Carter spins around on one while we order our usual: hamburgers for us and a hot dog for Carter.

We slide into a blue leatherette booth and move the chrome-topped salt and pepper shakers around in a game of chase on the gray Formica tabletop with a pink boomerang pattern. From the kitchen comes the sound of a radio cowboy singing about something he's lost—love, cows (we aren't quite sure).

When our lunch comes, the plates mounded with home fries, we taste why the parking lot is so crowded. We have to make the usual admonishment: hot dog first, fries later. Carter deftly pulls her hotdog from the bun and eats it in four bites, then digs into the french fries. I have to agree, crispy fries are much more interesting than a soft, white bun. Sucking on the peppermints that come with our bill, we head up the Mirror Lake Highway into the mountains.

By the time we find our favorite campground, nestled beneath a stand of Ponderosa pines at the edge of the Provo River, Carter has fallen asleep. I roll down the windows of the car and settle myself at the campsite's picnic table.

Bob picks his way up the boulders that line the rushing stream, being careful that his shadow does not frighten trout that might be lurking beneath a root or a rock ledge. Cadis flies dance above the burbling water.

He steadies himself on two large rocks and sets about casting. His fly lights on the water and floats rapidly downstream toward the still, dark pool shadowed by a tall spruce. The fly slows, then suddenly disappears as a fish draws it down. Bob gives a short tug and the line breaks free. He frowns and reels it back in. He tries to mimic the motions of an underwater bug by twitching his line as he pulls it toward him. No luck.

Bob reels in the fly, shakes it dry, then climbs a bit higher and begins to cast again. Forward and back, forward and back. With each cast he lets out six feet of line until the long, amber filament traces a graceful S against the blue autumn sky. With the last cast, he throws his arm out in front of him; the fly and line flow elegantly through the air and land gently on the water's smooth surface.

A silver flash breaks the quiet of the pool. A large trout arcs into the air, droplets of water sparkling all around it like a shower of diamonds. It's huge, two pounds at least. The fish dives on the fly and disappears. The line races out.

Behind Bob, the river forces its way through a tumble of boulders; the spray of the little waterspout mists the air. High above the waterfall, the mountains look as though someone has spread an oriental carpet over them, so bright are they with autumn's colors. The gold of the aspen and the red of the maple stand in sharp contrast to the deep green of the lodgepole pines, the cedars, and the spruce. At home it is still summer, but here in the mountains, fall has already begun.

Carter's sleepy face appears at the car window. I unbuckle her from her seat belt and settle her in my lap as she rubs her eyes. "Look," I whisper. "Granbob's caught a fish." She stares in fascination at her grandfather who is silhouetted against the autumn sky. He raises his rod high above him and reels in the line, pauses, then reels again.

"Is it a big one?" Carter asks me.

"Could be," I respond.

"Big as mine?" she asks again.

"Oh no," I say. "Not that big."

She snuggles down, content to watch her grandfather fish.

Bob leans down to reach for the trout and catches sight of Carter in my lap. He wiggles his rod in a wave. Carter waves back. He slips his hand into the water then stands up, shrugging his shoulders and smiling. "He got away," he calls down to us.

"That's all right, Granbob," Carter calls back. "We still have mine. I'll share."

All the way home, Carter chatters brightly from the backseat about her fish and the bait we used and how next time we might use that sparkly pink stuff . . . or maybe worms. She and Bob discuss just how to cook the fish. This time, she says, she's going to eat it up, every single bite, but assures Bob that she will give him some to make him feel better about losing his.

While Bob puts away the car, Carter and I take her fish inside. Her little sister, Mason, wants to play with it. Her parents are suitably impressed. "I got the biggest one there," Carter says proudly.

Then she lowers her voice. "But be nice to Granbob," she cautions them. " 'Cause his got away."

YOUR OWN FISHIN' HOLE

Make several construction paper fish and put a paper clip on the mouth of each. Your child can color them if she wishes, drawing in eyes, gills, and scales. Next, find a stick about three feet long (a yardstick or dowel will do), and tie a string about two feet long to one end. Attach a magnet to the end of the string. Place the fish in a bucket or wastebasket and let your little fisherman dangle her pole into the bucket and catch a fish. You can also make a game of this by writing numbers on the fish. Two or more children can play. The one whose fish add up to the highest total wins.

The Golden Thimble

Henderson Baker's hay and feed store is nestled in a hollow in the Blue Ridge Mountains. Toward the back of the store, behind the feed sacks, is a dusty spot where people leave things for him to sell. That's where I first spotted the old sewing machine.

"When did you get this in, Henderson?" I called out from the dim corner.

"Sally Harris brought it by last month," he replied. "Said she found it in her uncle's barn up near Red Hill."

I love these old machines, especially their ornate, cast-iron bases. We put two of them together to make our breakfast table. Another serves as a nightstand, combined with a marble top I rescued from a drawerless bureau. With old sewing machines the bases are usually the only part that is salvageable. The one in Henderson's store appeared to be no exception. The veneer was peeling and the drawers had been stripped of their brass pulls, but I knew that once the base was scraped, painted a glossy black, and topped with a piece of slate, it would make a perfect porch table. Henderson helped me load it onto my truck.

Back in my workshop, I lifted up the cover to the cabinet and had to catch my breath. Tucked away safely inside was the original machine. Its shiny black enamel and intricate gold ornamentation were in pristine condition. A wooden spool of thread was still in place. Its leather cable hung limply from the drive wheel. With a screwdriver, I slipped the belt back in place before adjusting the tension. Then I pulled up an old barrel, sat down, gingerly placed my foot on the treadle, and pressed down lightly. The machine still worked! A few drops of oil later, it began a contented whir as I pumped the treadle.

Looking for a scrap of fabric, I pried open one of the drawers. It contained a length of muslin, carefully wrapped around pieces of eyelet lace and blue ribbons. Beneath the muslin, a wooden darning egg nestled in some khaki-green socks whose heels still needed attention. A little pincushion, with a cross-stitched design of a ladybug on the top, bristled with needles and pins like a rusty porcupine.

I opened the other drawer, which held a half-knit child's sweater and, beneath it, a bundle of papers tied with red yarn. I carefully undid the little packet and spread out yellowed newspaper clippings, old letters, and faded photographs on my worktable. Among the pictures was a studio portrait of a handsome young man resplendent in a First World War uniform. A sepia photograph revealed a curly-haired toddler holding tightly to someone's leg. Another photo—taken a few years later—captured the child's dimpled smile and her dark curls caught up in a big bow. She was dressed in a white pinafore, edged in eyelet, and was pushing a china doll in a wicker baby carriage.

One newspaper clipping announced the marriage of Miss Adeline Booth to Mr. Emery Thackery on October 3, 1912. Another told of the departure of the Red Hill Guards to service in France in August of 1917. Several letters written to "Addie" by Emery described the beauty of France and the horrors of war. He closed each letter with "be sure to kiss little Emmie for me."

Leafing through the papers, I came upon an invitation to an American Library Association meeting and two ticket stubs to *The Nutcracker* in Richmond. I also discovered a poem in childish handwriting and a first-grade report card dated June 6, 1920. A Miss Emma Thackery had earned A's in penmanship, reading, and geography, and B's in arithmetic and citizenship.

As I closed the bottom drawer, a sock got caught. I jerked it free, and a little red leather case flew out and landed on the floor. Carefully opening it, I discovered a small golden thimble with the letters E.W.T. to A.E.B. engraved around its base. It glittered in the palm of my hand.

The next morning, I went to the Historical Society on Court House Square to try to find the Thackery family. In the newspaper file, I learned that the Red Hill Guards had returned from France "much decorated, to a hero's welcome on the station platform" on January 23, 1919. Eleven names were listed as returning; Emery's was not among them.

Over at the courthouse, I found the records of Adeline and

Emery's marriage and the birth of their daughter, Emma Marie. Emery was listed as a farmer. In the file of death certificates, one read: "Emery Wallace Thackery, age 31, died at Côte de Chatillon, France, on October 16, 1918." The war ended less than a month later. The last Thackery to graduate from the high school had done so in 1931. A search of the current phonebook for Thackerys proved fruitless.

I sighed in frustration. Then I remembered the invitation to the Library Association's meeting and went home to write them to see if Adeline had ever been a member. Two months later, a pale blue envelope arrived in my mailbox from the association's secretary. She told me that Mrs. Emery Thackery had been a member of their society from 1911 until 1962 and had been the librarian at a private girls' school in Virginia's Tidewater.

I made a quick phone call to the school and explained my quest to the headmistress. Mrs. Thackery had been a much-beloved member of the school staff, the headmistress told me, but she had died in 1978. Hearing the disappointment in my voice, she told me that Adeline's daughter was an alumna. Emma had married a Mr. Paul Hillman and lived in a town only eight miles from my home! I hung up the phone, smiling with satisfaction.

I looked up Mrs. Hillman's number and made another call. When I told her about the papers and the little thimble, she graciously invited me to her home for tea. A few days later, I pulled up at the Hillman home and knocked on the door. A young woman whose curly, dark hair and round face resembled the little girl in the faded photograph opened the front door.

"Hello," she smiled. "I'm Emily Lloyd; my grandmother is expecting you."

When I saw her, I knew at once that Mrs. Hillman had most certainly been the child in the photographs in the sewing machine cabinet. The curls were now silver, but her round cheeks still dimpled when she smiled. She took my hand and drew me down beside her on the sofa. I carefully spread out the little packet of papers and explained how I had found them.

Reaching for the photograph of the little girl in the pinafore, she said, "Here I am on my fifth birthday. My father sent me that doll from France." Then she touched the photograph of the soldier and said quietly, "And this was my father." Picking up the picture of the toddler she added, "This was me, and I think those are his legs for, you see,"—she pointed to the kneesocks—"those were part of his uniform. He left for the war when I was four and died in France."

I nodded, then asked, "Do you remember him, Mrs. Hillman?"

"Emma, please," she corrected me gently and continued, "Just little things, really. I can recall the sweet scent of his pipe and the feel of his tweed jacket against my cheek. He always kept peppermints in his pocket and let me find one there every evening after dinner."

I reached into my pocket and gently placed the red-leather case in Emma's hand. She opened it slowly and placed the thimble on her finger. It glimmered softly in the late afternoon light.

"Mother cherished this and always kept it in her jewelry box. But when we moved, it vanished," she said. "It was Father's wedding gift to her."

Emily brought in tea and admired the little thimble, as I told them how I had found the sewing machine. I related my search for the sewing machine's owner, the piecing together of clues, the letters, and the phone calls.

"How well I recall that wonderful machine," Emma said wistfully. "I used to think it was magic; Mother could make anything on it. Anything! All I had to do was admire a dress in a store window, and she would make one just like it for me—better actually. My dolls had wardrobes fit for a queen."

She reached for a photograph. "I'm sure she made this pinafore. And that doll had a wardrobe that would make a princess jealous." She continued with a laugh, "How I loved playing beneath the machine and pushing the treadle up and down—even though I got scolded for doing so!"

"When did you last see it?" I asked.

"Well," Mrs. Hillman thought a moment, "after Father died, Mother tried running the farm with some help from her brother, but she just couldn't make a go of it. When the school offered her a job as a librarian and housemother complete with rooms for us and a scholarship for me, she sold the farm to our neighbor. Our quarters were so tiny, we just didn't have room for the sewing machine, and so she had to leave it behind."

"I can deliver it to you tomorrow," I said suddenly. "It works just fine."

"No, no," Emma said, shaking her head. "I wouldn't hear of such a thing. The thimble and photographs are enough."

"But you must take it," I said. "It really doesn't belong to me. When I think of the special occasions it was used for, the lovely things it created, I cannot keep it. The memories are yours, not mine."

She hesitated. "Besides," I concluded, "I only wanted the base, not the machine. I can always find another."

"Thank you," Emma said softly. "That would be lovely." Then she smiled and said, "Emily is getting married this fall." Turning to her granddaughter, she asked, "Wouldn't it be wonderful if we could make your wedding dress on Mother's old sewing machine?"

Emily hugged her grandmother with delight. Then she poured us a second cup of tea and begged Emma to tell her more about her great-grandmother. As rain pattered gently against the windows, we listened to Emma's tales of her mother and of her tireless effort to run a farm—she, a city girl from Richmond. Emma told us of her mother's love of books and her determination to be a librarian in an age when women didn't usually have careers.

And she spoke of her mother's patience in teaching her the art of sewing. "A precious gift," she reflected. "One I have always treasured."

A few weeks ago, Emily and her fiancé came to fetch the sewing machine. Yesterday, the postman arrived at my door with a small parcel. I opened it to find a beautiful quilted tea cozy and matching napkins with hand-crocheted edges. The little note that was tucked in the box read, simply, "Thank you. From Emma (and Adeline)."

Needles and Pins

A pincushion is an easy first sewing project for a child. Simply cut two squares of fabric, about four inches on each side. Join the squares, right sides together, then sew around three sides and halfway down the fourth with small stitches. Now turn the square inside out, press it flat, and fill it with fiberfill or cotton batting.

If your child is able, one of the squares could be embroidered before putting the two pieces together. I have a lovely pincushion that my youngest daughter made for me one Mother's Day. On the top, in long, wobbly stitches, is the word Mom surrounded by little flowers. Sarah gave it to me twenty years ago. I still use it every day.

Migrations

I t is unusually warm for March. The window in my study is open and soft breezes blow the curtains. Suddenly, I hear a distant noise; the sound is unmistakable. Geese. As the faint honking grows cacophonous, I look out the window above my desk and search the patch of sky above our woods. I know I will soon see the graceful birds as they make their approach, gliding in for a landing on the pond at the bottom of the hill. They are heading home.

In a slightly ragged V, fifteen geese drift across the pale, spring sky. I've been expecting them. The sound of their honking always stirs something in me, a longing, a yearning for my own ancestral home, miles to the north.

As I turn back to work, my eye falls on the large glass lamp casting a pool of yellow light on my desk. For as long as I can remember, I've returned from my grandparents' home on Cape Cod each summer with a small bit of the seashore: a chunk of sea glass, a shell, a small piece of driftwood. My lamp is filled with these treasures. The paperweight that attempts to keep my pile of manuscripts orderly is a large whelk shell.

I put the shell to my ear and listen to whispering waves breaking on the sand. The summer I found it thrown high against the dunes by a winter storm I was about ten, the age when children begin to change from merely observing Nature to longing to know more about it. When we returned from the beach, I ran to show my grandmother my new treasure. She was where I knew she would be, in the garden behind her rambling old house. From its high terrace, she could look out across the tidal river, which nourished the life of the marsh. She had recently begun to show me the complex community of watery life that dwelled in the shadows of the dock and among the stiff marsh grasses—a community, she told me, that depended upon the ebb and flow of the tides.

In her lap she had her ever-present binoculars, the ones she used to watch the birds that darted among high branches of the linden tree, or sipped nectar from her flowers. That summer she taught me the birds' names and how to distinguish their calls; she spoke of their long winter flights and how they returned each spring to their summer home—just as I did.

When I showed her my shell and told her I had heard the ocean in it, she smiled and said that, in a way, I was right. But, she explained, it was the ocean inside me that I heard, the essence of my life in the world, the exaggerated throbbing of my own heart, the whispering of my blood. The shell might have come from a long way off, she said. When I had asked if it might have come from as far away as the birds flew for the winter, she nodded.

Perhaps it was those summers by the river, on the marsh, along the shore, that helped form my belief that a woman's life is like the seasons. We reflect the slow cadence of nature's cycles. In our ability to create life and then nourish that life, we are like the sea itself from whose waters this world of ours once emerged. The sound we hear in a seashell is the same sound our children hear during the long months before their birth.

Each spring, as I watch the sky above my home fill with birds returning from their winter havens, I feel the pull of the shore. The rhythm of the season quickens. I become part of the migration and, like the generations before me, begin making plans for my summer by the sea.

I am not alone. Many of my friends speak of a special place that they, too, think of as their spiritual home. It may be a cabin by a lake, a little motel by the seashore, a campsite by a rushing stream, a lodge in a national park. It may be a house that has been in their family for generations, or just a spot to which they always return, every year or as often as they can. For all of us, no matter how often we have moved, how far away we have lived from family, these places are part of our roots. They nourish our souls.

Now I have grandchildren of my own. Like my own children, they will hear the stories of the past, learn about the life of the sea, and the birds, and the land. In them, the cycle of life begins anew.

Through the open window, I can hear the contented noises of the geese settling in for the evening. As I begin writing letters to my children, inviting them to our own annual migration, my gaze falls upon my shell. Perhaps, this summer one of my granddaughters will find a shell like mine. And, when she holds it to her ear, she will hear the sound that has always drawn me back to the shore. The sound of the sea and of summer and of the secret sounds deep within herself.

MIGRATIONS—THE GAME

Birds (and people) migrate, but so do all sorts of other creatures: salmon, turtles, butterflies, elephants, caribou, zebras, whales, and many more. Discuss with your children the many things that animals, fish, and birds might encounter on their annual journeys. What helps them? What hinders?

Turn an old board game into a migration game. Choose your species, create game pieces that look like them, and have the board represent their trip from your hometown or area to their winter home. Research the challenges faced by your species and make some cards that represent potential disasters (or benefits). Roll the dice and move your piece ahead. If you land on a marked square, you have to pick a card that might set you back (or ahead) 100 miles. For instance, some of the dangers a Monarch butterfly could face might be eating too much milkweed or encountering plants sprayed with pesticide. The butterfly could be eaten by a bird, blown off course, or netted by a collector. First butterfly to reach its special tree in Mexico wins!

A First Time for Fireflies

I n the gathering twilight, furtive figures dart across the lawn. The song of the peepers and the katydids is accompanied by excited shouts of "Got one!" or "Quick, Daddy, catch it."

Our granddaughter, Carter, has discovered fireflies. In my own naïveté, I thought everyone knew what a firefly was. I was sure that, come summer, each and every town in America was decorated by the twinkling of their night-time flights. But I was wrong.

On the first evening of their annual visit to our home in Virginia's Piedmont, we were sitting on the porch, lingering at the table after dinner, when suddenly Carter gasped, "Oh look, a shooting star!" Then, gazing about in confusion, she said, "And another one. And another."

We looked where she was pointing and saw the fireflies blinking their Morse code of love. In an instant, Carter was out of her chair, chasing the twinkling bugs and squealing in delight. Her little sister, Mason, sitting in her mother's lap, clapped her dimpled hands and cooed with pleasure. Our son, Drew, ran to join his daughter, saying, "I'd forgotten about the fireflies."

I turned to my daughter-in-law, who was smiling at the excitement of her family. "You don't have fireflies in Utah?" Jill shook her head. Of course not, I realized. Fireflies spend the day in the cool, damp grass. Then, when darkness begins to fall, they emerge into the coolness of evening and begin their courtship dance. Slowly, they rise to the tops of the trees, where they garland the branches like tiny ropes of twinkling diamonds. Utah is mostly desert. It is hot and dry, and there is no cool, deep grass for the fireflies.

During her visit with us, Carter has been busy discovering all the differences between our home and hers. "Let's walk down the hill to the pond," I suggested to Carter on the first day of her visit. She looked up at me, perplexed, and said, "This isn't a hill, Gammy!"

I laughed, as I realized that the gently rolling landscape of the Blue Ridge Piedmont is a far cry from the majestic Wasatch Mountains that surround her home in Utah. Accustomed to walking up her steep driveway, she ran right up our sloping one in thirty seconds flat, leaving me, the lowlander, puffing far behind. Everything here is new and different. Carter and Mason do not have Canada geese that honk loudly as they come in for a landing on the pond or a white horse who, with his two donkey friends, pokes his head over the fence, looking for handouts of carrots and apples. And they don't have fireflies.

Why is that that which we know, that which we have lived, we think to be the province of all people? When I went away to school, I was astonished that everyone there did not know how to sew. That was just part of growing up, I thought. Everyone learned how to sew. But most of my classmates had not. My surprise gave way to pleasure as I quickly discovered that I could earn spending money by mending and altering things for the other women in my dorm. I even began a small business making the A-line jumpers that were all the rage when combined with black tights and a turtleneck.

Over the years, I have discovered that assumptions can get me into trouble. I try to remember not to express surprise when others' lives and experiences do not match my own. I do not always succeed. In my enthusiasm for learning more about other people and different cultures, I sometimes rush pell-mell into conversations, without thinking. I'm working on that. So is our youngest daughter.

"You've never seen snow?" Sarah asked incredulously of her fellow teachers, her first week at a boarding school in Mobile, Alabama. Several shook their heads no.

"Astonishing," she murmured, as they helped each other move into the faculty apartments. "Well," one young woman said, her arms full of books, "It did snow a little bit when I was a kid. But I was asleep, and it was gone before I woke up."

Two years later, when Sarah moved to New York, her friend Scott offered to help her drive her U-Haul. "Maybe I'll get to see snow," he said, hopefully. Their plan was to make their first stop at our house. The night they arrived, it was sleeting heavily. The driveway was a sheet of ice. They got a running start and made it up the hill, then collapsed in exhaustion after sixteen hours of driving. When Scott awoke around noon the next day, five inches of fresh snow covered the ground with its soft whiteness. More was falling.

Sarah was ecstatic. "Do we still have a sled?" she asked eagerly. Of course we had a sled. No one gives away a sled. You never know when you might need one.

What fun it was to watch those two squeeze themselves onto a tiny red toboggan and career down the hill. "Remember to bail out at the bottom," I called after them. "The pond's not frozen yet."

They sledded for half an hour, then made snow angels. A snowball fight and snowmen-making ensued. Looking out the frosted windows, I saw Scott catching snowflakes on his tongue. Just as my children had done, just as I had done before them. He was as excited as—well, as excited as Carter chasing her first fireflies.

What a pleasure it is to see someone experience a first joy or a new discovery. When our daughter Eleanor was a senior in high school, she spent the academic year in a little French village near Lyons. She wrote home of finally conquering the language, making friends, learning how to make cookies called *langue de chat*. Our Christmas present to her that year was an airplane ticket for her French "sister," Véronique, to come and visit us that summer. Véro had never been out of the Loire Valley.

"*Quelle gros voiture*," she said in amazement, when we picked her up at the airport in our ordinary, American sedan. It was billed as a mid-size car, but it looked huge to her. And then we all laughed, Véro included, as her eyes grew big as saucers when a stretch limo drove by.

For a month, we saw our country through French eyes. Véro loved American food (although Eleanor was, by now, looking down her nose at it), thought having a little sister was *chouette*, and that hot dogs were equally cool. She was astonished by the size of our supermarkets and wished our American movies had French subtitles.

As a hostess present, Véro had brought us a tin of dried chanterelles that she and her parents had gathered in the woods of the Haute Loire. She showed me how to make *potage aux champignons* with them. I'd never made anything with dried mushrooms before, soup included, which surprised her, too. Now, her version of mushroom soup is one of my favorite recipes.

This evening, as I watch Drew show his daughter how to gently cup her hands around the glimmering fireflies, I reflect on the sense of wonder that children have, that we all have, actually, when confronted with something new and wonderful.

Tomorrow, Carter will have her very first ride on a pony. Our neighbor has a gentle brown mare named Montana, who, he says, can't wait to have a little girl on her back. I must look and see if I still have that old cowboy hat that Drew loved to wear when he was about Carter's age.

Drew races to the porch. "Have you got a bug jar, Mom?" he asks.

I know why he wants it. He and Carter will put a few fireflies in the jar and add some grass and a stick for climbing. And maybe, as he and his sisters used to do, they will add a little bottle cap full of water, in case the fireflies get thirsty in the middle of the night. The jar will rest by Carter's bed, and she will slowly slip off to sleep, watching Nature's nightlight softly glowing on the bedside table.

I know I've got a jar in the back of the cupboard somewhere—a peanut butter jar with lots of holes poked in the lid.

"Mom?" Drew asks again, bringing me back to the present.

"Of course, I have a jar," I laugh. "You never throw away a bug jar; you never know when you might need it."

He smiles, and suddenly I am not looking at my six-foot-three son but his three-foot-six former self who asked that same question so many years ago. First-time discoveries are wonderful. Second-time rediscoveries are pretty good, too.

CREEPY CRAWLIES

It's great fun to watch creepy crawly things up close. With a bug jar, you can have your own private view into the world of insects. Just find a clean jar with a screw top—glass is fine, but plastic might be safer, should it be dropped. Punch about a dozen holes in the lid and fill it with a bit of grass, several leaves, a stick or two, and a few drops of water. Now, catch your bug. Slugs and snails make fine temporary pets, too. Their slow progress across the glass is fascinating to watch. Winged or not, big or small, most bugs will do fine for a day in a jar. Just be sure to keep it out of direct sunlight and don't forget to let your critters out after twenty-four hours.

The Heart of the Home

That children should be seen and not heard was a widely accepted opinion of the Gilded Age. All along New York's Fifth Avenue, on Beacon Hill in Boston, and up and down Millionaire's Row in Pittsburgh, the children of the country's wealthiest families were routinely relegated to the care of nannies. They rarely ate meals with their parents and seldom accompanied the adults of their families on trips or vacations. Often, for afternoon teas, the children might be dressed up, briefly introduced to their parents' friends, and then whisked back to the nursery—a room usually located in a separate wing, far removed from their parents' bedrooms. Like the latest-model carriage or a Worth gown from Paris, for many captains of industry, children were just another fashion accessory.

Not so the children of Pittsburgh steel magnate Henry Clay Frick and his wife, Adelaide. Their Pennsylvania home, Clayton, was "the happiest of places," wrote their daughter, Helen, of the elegant Victorian mansion that was her home, on and off, for over ninety years. After a long career in philanthropy, Helen returned to Clayton and made it her permanent home. There, she loved to entertain her older brother Childs' children, grandchildren, and great-grandchildren, who called her Granti, their abbreviation for "great auntie." At her death in 1984, Helen Clay Frick left her "dear old house" to the American people, so we might glimpse a world where children were the heart of the home.

The first painting today's visitors to Clayton see when they enter the stately home is a charming portrait of a young girl with a toddler seated in her lap. The Fricks placed this artwork in the foyer to symbolize the central position their children had in their lives. The painting is but one of many subtle signs that the Fricks were not typical Victorian-era parents and that young Childs, Martha, and Helen were an intimate part of their parents' busy world.

While an impressive European and American art collection fills the house, on the deep red cut-velvet walls of Mrs. Frick's bedchamber and on every available surface of Mr. Frick's bedroom, photographs of their son and daughters are on display. Far from being banished to fourth-floor bedrooms, the children slept in a nursery connected to their mother's room by a private bath. The sunny nursery walls are festooned with painted garlands and flowers; images of cheerful bluebirds dart across the ceiling. Three little brass beds line one wall.

Child-sized furniture is everywhere, for no room at Clayton was off limits. Next to the back door is a tiny sink where the children would wash their hands after hanging their cloaks on low, butterfly-shaped hooks. A faded kite still hangs beside the coat tree.

With over ninety percent of its original furnishings still present, Clayton looks much as it did at the turn of the century. The family's second-floor sitting room brims with books and games, cards and toys. The classroom on the fourth floor, where the children were taught by their governess, evokes scenes of lively lessons. The cozy windowseat at the top of the massive staircase was the children's favorite perch from which to watch the captains of industry and their elegantly gowned wives sweep into the home for festive occasions, perhaps catching a wink from men like Andrew Carnegie or Teddy Roosevelt.

Last spring, while strolling through the grounds, I came upon a wonderful bench hidden beneath a rose-covered arbor that arched above the path to the children's playhouse (this little building was designed with small, intimate rooms and even had a bowling alley for rainy-day amusement). As I rested in the rose-scented shadows, I watched a young mother chatting with a friend on the nearby path. Engaged in animated conversation, she ignored her son's tugs at her sleeve. Finally, she put her finger to her lips. Sighing, the little boy sunk down onto the grass. When one lives in the land of children, a bit of adult conversation is a bright spot. You wonder if you will ever be able to finish a sentence, read a book, have a bit of time for yourself. I remember.

In the early years of our marriage, when my husband, Bob, and I lived in New York City, Central Park was our oasis in the midst of the bustle of Manhattan. Frederick Law Olmstead designed it to be a retreat for all. In 1913, when Henry Clay Frick built his imposing mansion right across from its sweeping lawns and towering trees, the park was the place to be seen. Families promenaded along its pathways in their Sunday best, and children launched kites in the former pasture still known as the Sheep Meadow.

As soon as our son, Drew, could toddle, we took him on weekly trips to play in the park. We passed Mr. Frick's home often. By then, it had been a museum and library for thirty years. Little did I realize that, when my toddler had gone off to college, I would begin a new career as an art historian and return to the Frick to research my first book.

When Bob finished graduate school, we left New York and had two daughters. There was little time for my own interests when the children were small. I thought that was how it would always be, but I was wrong.

Back at Clayton, the little boy was beginning to fidget, and it became his mother's turn to sigh. Breaking off her conversation, she rolled her eyes at her friend, helped her son to his feet, and they set off together across the broad lawn. It is hard, when you are little, to understand why the person who is the center of your universe cannot give all her time to you. It is hard, too, when one is in the midst of mothering, to believe that the intensity of children's needs will ever lessen.

But they do. Our children are all grown and gone now. We have three grandchildren—and we are remembering, once again, the importance of patience.

"Have patience," I wanted to call out after the retreating figures. "There will be time." At a historic home like Clayton, one can see that clearly. The decades have passed, the family is gone, yet there is a timeless quality to the place as though it is still waiting for the family to return, for the children to once again fill the nursery with laughter.

As I sit by the playhouse, I think of the beautiful painting of Helen Frick and her father that hangs in the National Portrait Gallery in Washington. That this titan of industry chose to have his daughter included in his official portrait has always fascinated me. Clearly his children never surrendered their rightful place in his heart. We cannot recapture the past; only in art and in museums does time stand still. However, we can hope that, when we look back in time, our memories will be rich and happy ones.

Index